AUSTRALIAN VOICES IN PRINT

PROMOTING POPULAR AUSTRALIAN AUTHORS.

My Mother's Ways

❖

My Mother's Ways

Being a book of household hints
from the early 1900s
in Australia

Collected and with an introduction
by Mary Murray

MALLON PUBLISHING

Produced by Mallon Publishing

First published 1996 by Mallon Publishing Pty Limited
PO Box 375, Clifton Hill, Vic 3068

Reprinted 1997, 1999, 2002, 2010

Printed and bound in Singapore by Tien Wah Press (Pte.) Ltd

Design, layout and typesetting: Pauline Deakin, Captured Concepts

Managing Editor: Kathleen Rushford

Editor: Ev Beisebarth

National Library of Australia
Cataloguing-in-Publication data
My mother's ways: being a book of household hints
from the early 1900s in Australia.
ISBN 9781875696024
1. Home economics – Australia. I. Murray, Mary,
640.410994

Contents

❖

Acknowledgements

❖

The publisher and author gratefully acknowledge the McDonald, Shedden, O'Brien, Rushford, Porter and O'Connell families for generously allowing their photographs to be reproduced in this book. Thanks are also extended to Fleur Toone for picture research and manuscript preparation in the early stages, and to Joan Macfarlane, Kane Jarrods Photography, Mary Costello, Lee White and David Deakin for their contributions.

The illustrations on pages ii-iii, 60 (bottom), 92, 103, 105, 108, 109, 111, 115, 120, 123, 131, 136, 139, 145, 149 and 150, and on the cover are reproduced with the permission of the Mitchell Library, State Library of NSW, from the Small Pictures File and their collections GPO 1 and At Work and Play. The illustrations on pages 19, 22, 27, 35 and 121 are from The Biggest Family Album in Australia, Museum of Victoria, Scienceworks Collection.

Introduction

❖

Things my mother taught me

The idea for this book came to me when my sister, Eve, (who has since passed away), said to me, 'Mary, our lives were shaped by the things our mother taught us – by her wonderful ideas, her wisdom and knowledge, her graciousness and compassion.'

The hints and ideas in this collection belong to a time and a generation of Australian women when making the best of things, living within one's means, turning one's hands to any task and lending a helping hand to others were the accepted practices of everyday life. It was a time when reusing and recycling were prompted as much by practical necessity as by gratitude for the bounty of the land, when women kept their families in good health, and well fed and clothed, with home-grown food and hand-made garments.

My own mother never owned a refrigerator; she had an ice chest and before that a Coolgardie safe, yet she kept her food safe and healthy for her family of eleven without the scientific gadgetry we take for granted today. Hers was the 'making do' generation. Having little, she wanted little and was content with what she had. Yet in many ways her life was richer than many in this day and age, being wealthy in practical wisdom, prudent management and generosity of spirit and action. Her generation passed on a relatively clean world to us, returning to the earth only that which was wholesome and regenerative.

These household hints evoke the wide range and diversity of interests, occupations and responsibilities of the women of my mother's era, as well as the creative, often ingenious use they made of the ordinary, humble and familiar materials at hand in the home. Most of these items are just as readily available to us and their past uses are worthy of imitation and as relevant in application today as then.

This book is dedicated to my own dear departed mother for teaching me through her example, and to all my relatives, friends and acquaintances who have kept alive the ideas and ideals of the past in their daily practices, as well as in their collections of hints, recipes and memorabilia from our youthful days.

Mary Murray
Scarborough, 1995

Children

❖

Although children in those days had various jobs to perform and responsibilities around the farm or in the house, they were still greatly cherished and cared for. Rearing families of eight to ten was not uncommon, and managing to bring up healthy and happy children was the aim then as now. The resourceful mother of such a brood was always on the lookout for ways to make the best use of limited resources, as the hints in this chapter show.

Keeping a large family properly dressed, well fed and amused was of prime concern, and practical ways of making much out of little were essential in achieving that aim. Toys and entertainments for children were created out of items readily to hand. Costumes for parties were made at home, as were inexpensive treats and novelties for special occasions. Practical and long-lasting clothes were made attractive with trimmings and braids, and numerous ways of tempting children's appetites with nourishing food were devised by these skilled household managers.

Always keep the legs of old flannelette pyjamas; they make excellent linings for little boys' trousers for winter wear.

❖

Don't throw away the cuffs of white gloves; they make very pretty collars for small girls' dresses.

❖

Replace the worn ends of a boy's braces with pieces cut from the tongue of an old boot or shoe. Lasts well.

❖

Give your children a healthy milk drink by mashing a ripe banana with a small teaspoon of sugar, gradually adding 1/2 pint of chilled milk. Beat with a rotary beater until frothy and serve quickly before the banana discolours.

❖

Make your boy a serviceable pair of overalls. Boil two sugar bags, cut along the seams and press, then dye them a dark brown or navy blue. Good for backyard romping.

❖

It's a good idea to make children's sun-hats from unbleached calico. Bind with coloured bias-binding and machine round and round the brim, first putting 'ingrain' cotton in the shuttle to match the hat. They wash well and can be starched to the required stiffness.

A barometer which children can make is made as follows. You need a 1/2-pint bottle and a 1 pound glass jar. The bottle must stand comfortably upside down in the jar. Half-fill the bottle with water, adding a few drops of red ink or other colouring matter. Place jar upside down on top of the bottle and reverse, allowing the water to flow into the jar until only an inch or two of water remains in the neck of the bottle. The column of water rises when fine weather is indicated and drops when rain or fierce wind is to be expected. Good for boys to make.

When putting a bar in the children's cupboard, nail at each end vertical boards with four or five holes in them. As the clothes grow longer as the children age, the bar can be raised to suit the length. Remember, you are dealing with 'little people' who are using adult-sized furniture.

❖

When making a paste of flour and water (good for children to use) add 1 teaspoon of gelatine dissolved in a little hot water. Mix it well and the paste will be very smooth.

❖

Here is a nice idea for icing a cake for a children's party. Ice the cake in the usual way, and then with a different coloured icing mark the cake into as many sections as there are to be children and write each child's name in one of the sections.

❖

Before commencing to knit baby garments, dust the hands with lavender powder; the woollies will have a delightful fragrance when finished.

❖

Sew two buttons on the children's house slippers, then paint them with luminous paint. The youngsters will have no trouble finding their slippers in the dark – in fact, they enjoy looking for them.

❖

When making or buying new overalls or frocks for children, sew tape round the underarm seams. This will prevent any tears when they reach upwards in play.

❖

Knit your own 'chain mail' jerkin. You will need silver-grey wool and a pair of coarse needles. Make the whole jerkin in plain knitting and give it a light coat of silver paint. If staging a medieval play, or if school-children are staging Shakespeare, very realistic 'chain mail' can be achieved.

❖

You can mend celluloid or other pliable material toys by simply heating a fine steel knitting needle, placing the broken pieces together and placing the hot needle between them. The heat melts the pieces and sets immediately. Children have strong little hands, but with patience you can be Father Christmas over and over again by repairing.

When ice first came to our district, a boy of eleven or twelve had never seen it before and was so fascinated by it he took a piece and hid it for later. When he returned to get it and couldn't find it, he thought someone had stolen it from him!

❖

Children who dislike vegetables will very often take a soup made from vegetable, liquid, or pulped broth with a little Marmite dissolved in it. Very nourishing.

❖

When making little girls' tunics, sew half a press-stud on the underside of the shoulder-seam at the neck edge and the corresponding half on the outside of the blouse. Press together to ensure tidiness and comfort for the child with a non-slip shoulder-holder.

❖

After making sweet pies, roll out any surplus pastry into fancy shapes and bake. Served hot or cold with butter, jam or lemon cheese, this makes an appetising after-school treat.

❖

Keep a supply of waxed drinking-cups handy and whenever you are making desserts, including custard, blancmange, jellies, or gelatine-based puddings, pour some into the cups. Children love these little cups with their lunch.

Here is a use for baby's cot, when it's no longer needed for baby. A baby's cot will serve many purposes, but one of the most useful is a clothes horse. Take the four sides apart, hinge two equal parts together and make a pyramid of it. This makes an excellent clothes horse for drying clothes in front of the fire during winter. Attach a strap at the bottom to stop it from slipping. It can easily be converted back into a cot when needed.

To prevent a small child from pulling the laces out of his shoes, stitch the laces together at the place where they first cross. Even a sharp tug will fail to dislodge the laces, and it saves you endless time in re-lacing them.

❖

When making nighties for baby, allow an extra wide hem around the bottom. Put a drawstring or tape through the hem. It can be pulled up like a bag, and no matter how much baby kicks his or her legs they will never be uncovered in the cool weather.

The quality of stew will be much improved if rolled oats are used for thickening instead of the customary flour. Body-building for children!

❖

When making blancmange for a kiddies' party, add the pulp of two or three passionfruits and a few drops of cochineal to the mixture. Set in individual cups.

❖

For a healthful sweet, try these Banana Bingos. Cut peeled bananas cross-wise into 1-inch sections. Melt some sweet chocolate in the top of a double boiler, dip each piece of banana in chocolate and place in tiny wax paper cups. Insert a coloured toothpick in each piece and leave to harden. Good idea for a children's party.

For filling the bodies, limbs, etc., of home-made soft toys, use 'wood waste' – the fine string-like slivers used for packing crockery and the like, usually given away freely by most tradesmen. Toys firmly stuffed with this never get floppy or out of shape.

❖

If the youngsters are reluctant to wash themselves, try giving each of them a tablet of coloured soap and a fancy face-cloth.

Cut the best parts from your hubby's discarded cotton singlets and make your small boy a 'polo' shirt. It is quite a simple matter if you face the placket with bemberg or calico and bind the seams with tape. If using athletic-style singlets, make the collar from the broad shoulder-strap. The tiny shirts give long service.

If you dislike milk, add a teaspoon of golden syrup to each glass. This is a good plan if children are reluctant to drink milk; most will eagerly ask for it again, and you can gradually reduce the amount of syrup.

When needing to lengthen the kiddies' clothes you can eliminate a hem mark by making a solution of a cup of hot water, 1/2 teaspoon of vinegar and 1/4 teaspoon of borax. Mix well, wet a cloth with the solution, wring out, and place over the hem. Press on the wrong side until the cloth is practically dry. Leave the article to dry out completely and then brush to remove the powder. If colours are slightly different, run a coloured braid around the line of the 'let down'.

Roll out any left-over bread dough to about 1/2-inch thickness and bake in quick oven until brown and crisp. Cut into long fingers and split and butter while still hot. The children love them.

❖

If men's woollen scarves are no longer used, they can be made into skirts for small children two to three years old. The width of the scarf becomes the length; attach it to a bodice. If enough is left, make a little jerkin to match and decorate with braiding to suit.

❖

After ironing a little girl's pleated skirt slip a bobby-pin over each pleat until ready for wearing.

❖

Stir equal parts of honey and peanut butter together to form a paste and use for sandwich filling between slices of brown bread.

❖

Two nice multi-coloured bath-towels sewn together make a good warm wrap for baby about the house of a morning, and they are very easy to launder.

Cartoon strips from the newspaper pages pasted into an exercise book will provide many interesting hours for the young child. Give them crayons to colour the pictures.

❖

If your child has long straight hair and you put it in rags every night to encourage curling, dip your fingers into warm water in which a little gelatine has been dissolved as you put in each rag. Next morning the hair will curl beautifully for you.

❖

Get the stammering child to clench the teeth and talk through them whenever it feels unable to speak plainly. For some reason this method seems to inspire confidence, and if practised daily could lead to a permanent cure. Adults with a slight speech impediment will benefit also

❖

You may travel in comfort with baby in spite of railway restrictions on prams. Into a long, shallow, long-handled flower-basket, place a soft fluffy blanket and a baby pillow, and travel aboard the train in comfort. Mother carries the basket through her arm or at full-arm swing. In a bus or tram you can set the basket beside you on the seat and you are both free to enjoy the outing.

Fit a 'rear-vision' mirror to the pram. Not only can you see all that is taking place at the rear, but you can watch baby without having to bend over the hood.

Cookery &
Kitchen Tips

The kitchen, of course, was an entirely different place in the homes of the early 1900s. Coolgardie safes and wood-fired stoves were the refrigerators and ovens of the time, and the dishwashers, microwaves and other appliances of the modern era had no parallels. The recipes presented here reflect an era when cream, butter, eggs and meat were consumed in large quantities. Indeed, many households kept hens and other livestock. The pantry was well stocked with home-made preserves and cakes, and the vegetable garden and orchard provided bountiful produce.

Despite the quantities of fresh provisions that a household garden produced, much emphasis was placed on preserving food in the form of jams, jellies and chutneys. For the women of the era, waste was anathema, and many hints in this chapter reflect the economical uses of leftovers, and of dishes that, inexpensive to create, provided good nourishment for large families. Simple and practical ideas for saving time and money, as well as helpful tips on cleaning, re-using and substituting in the kitchen, can be found in this chapter, many of them equally useful today.

'Beggerman's Soup' takes some beating. Put all the cheese and bacon rinds available into a saucepan. Add pepper and salt, and a handful of breadcrumbs for each person, and milk and water to make the required quantity. Boil for about 40 minutes. Serve with large croutons. This will warm the 'cockles of your heart'!

❖

A different accompaniment for vegetable or meat broths for your next dinner-party! Add marble-sized balls of puff pastry to boiling soup five minutes before serving. Boil for two or three minutes until fluffy, and serve three or four in each soup dish.

❖

A delightful luncheon soup for that special ladies' 'get-together' Heat together a tin of mushroom soup, a tin of oyster soup, onion juice, the required amount of liquid made up of two-thirds milk and one-third water, pepper and salt. Heat slowly and do not boil. Water crackers are nice served with this.

❖

A hearty soup can be made with potatoes and onions. Boil required number of potatoes and onions together until tender. Remove from liquid and mash together, return to saucepan and keep warm. make a paste of 2 tablespoons flour, 2 tablespoons melted butter or margarine and 1 small cup of milk. Add gradually to mashed vegetables, avoiding lumps; season to taste and add chopped parsley.

❖

Add some peanut butter to soup which has been burnt by lentils or meat sticking to the bottom. Stir well before removing from heat. The burnt taste will be eliminated.

❖

Try parboiling tripe, then cut it into 3-inch squares and stuff with a mixture of herbs, breadcrumbs and seasonings. Roll in milk, then in breadcrumbs, and bake until golden brown. Serve with lemon wedges.

❖

When preparing meat or lamb cutlets, try rolling them in desiccated coconut instead of crumbs. The result is a tempting nutty flavour.

❖

Try mixing equal quantities of apricot jam and Worcestershire sauce together as a relish for corned mutton. It gives an entirely different flavour which is most appetising.

❖

When it is impossible to season a baked joint, roll the seasoning in greaseproof paper and bake it alongside.

❖

If corned brisket is scraggy, bone it, spread meat out flat, put several slices of bacon on it and roll up; tie firmly and boil in well-floured pudding cloth. Cooked this way the meat has a ham flavour and is easier to cut.

❖

One way to achieve crisp crackling on a leg of pork is to rub a little lemon juice over it before cooking. Another way is to cut deep scores in the skin and rub in finely chopped onion mixed with powdered sage and good seasonings. This lends additional savoury flavour.

Use milk – skimmed will do – for basting when roasting poultry. The result will be a delicious flavour and crisp skin.

❖

Sprinkle about a teaspoon of sugar in the baking-dish before putting in the roast meat; when the gravy is made it will be rich and brown.

❖

Next time you cook a ham, boil it for two-thirds of the cooking time, then spread it with treacle mixed with 2 tablespoons of mustard. Stick a few cloves into the ham, sprinkle with bread-crumbs, and bake in a moderate oven. Be sure the treacle doesn't burn. The combination of parboiling and baking to finish is delicious.

When roasting a fowl or rabbit in the oven, cover it with a greased cloth instead of greased paper. The cloth will not burn and can be easily lifted off when basting. A 25-pound flour-bag makes an ideal cloth.

If you have a chicken or duck which you cannot cook for a day or so, put an unpeeled onion inside the bird; this helps to keep poultry fresh until needed.

When roasting meat, turn joints with spoons instead of using a fork which pierces the meat and lets out the juices.

❖

When boiling a piece of corned beef or ham, add a tablespoon of treacle to the water. If you leave it in the water until cold it will cut tender and moist.

❖

Rabbit is delicious when cut into suitable portions, boiled in salted water until tender, drained, dipped in beaten egg and rolled in breadcrumbs, or dipped in batter with a pinch of herbs and a dash of Worcestershire sauce added. Fry until golden brown. Prepare chicken this way, too.

❖

For a tasty grill make a slot in a thick steak and fill it with oysters; sew up and grill for 15 minutes. Serve with a sauce made with a little cornflour and the beards of the oysters, a knob of butter about the size of a walnut, and a little stock. (Oysters were about one shilling a dozen way back then; or you collected your own off the rocks.)

❖

Those who live in the country and can get plenty of rabbits will find that rabbits' livers – two per adult – make a delectable dish and are so much more tender than sheep's livers. Kangaroos' livers are also a delicacy; remove the galls from both before cooking.

❖

When using meat recipes calling for frying, always remember to sprinkle the pan with salt before putting in fat. This prevents splashing, but does not over-flavour the meat.

❖

The shell of a hard-boiled egg will peel much easier if it is firmly rolled back and forth on the table before you attempt to peel it.

❖

A simple way to separate eggs is to break them one at a time into a small funnel. The whites will pass through, the yolks remain.

❖

Before frying slices of tomato, sprinkle them with a few drops of vinegar; it keeps them from breaking.

THE HOLBORN EGG WHISK

When a pumpkin is too large for one meal, rub bicarb soda into the cut surface and the remaining portion will keep good and fresh until wanted again.

❖

If you have a gas stove, or ring, take the skins from tomatoes by holding them one by one over the flame on the end of a long fork. This is quick and easy; the skins break and peel off easily and the job is less messy.

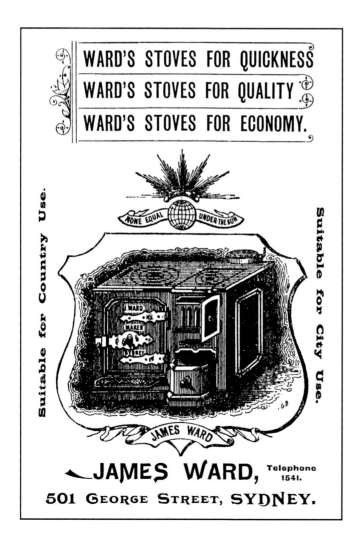

Don't throw away the water in which macaroni has been cooked. It makes a nice fine 'starch' for many things such as doileys or tray-cloths; for a thicker starch, save the water from boiled rice.

❖

Potatoes put into cold salted water for about fifteen minutes before putting into the oven to bake will cook in half the time, and will be well flavoured.

❖

Use rain water when making pea soup from dried split-peas. It takes twice as long for the peas to soften if hard water, or reservoir water, is used.

❖

Duck eggs used for custards or sponges will be much lighter if a tablespoon of boiling water is added to each egg.

❖

A teaspoon of flour added to the melted dripping in which eggs are to be fried will prevent the eggs from breaking or sticking to the pan.

❖

Strong white cotton thread drawn firmly across a hard-boiled egg will cut it into neat slices. This is a good tip if you don't possess a proper egg-slicer.

Try Swiss mountain eggs for something different. Melt a good dessertspoon of butter in a shallow dish and sprinkle with a thin layer of Gruyere cheese. Crack four eggs into the dish, and add seasoning and nutmeg to each egg. Pour in 3 tablespoons of cream, put a little more cheese on top and dot with butter. Bake for 15 minutes at moderate heat.

Mix half an ounce of celery seed with half a cup of brandy; steep for fourteen days, then strain and bottle. A few drops will flavour soup or stew and give one a reputation for 'French cooking'.

❖

If you inadvertently mixed boiled eggs with fresh ones, you can determine which are which by spinning them. The fresh ones will spin well, but the boiled ones will merely wobble about.

❖

Make a 1/2-pint of cream from a 1/4-pint, in this way. Empty the jar of cream into a basin, almost fill the jar with fresh milk and add this to the cream with a teaspoon of icing sugar. Whip with an egg-beater. The cream will beat up so thickly you'll have enough for two sandwich cakes, or the evening sweet course.

Dash a few drops of very cold water on to boiling milk, custard or milk coffee before taking it from the flame or fire. This keeps any skin from forming on top of the milk.

❖

Instead of salting the butter when making it, put the salt in the water in which it is being worked; the butter will never be streaky.

❖

PARROT PIE.

When whipping cream, sweeten it with honey, using a dessert-spoon to each 1/2-pint of cream. Do this, and the cream will remain thick all day.

❖

Brown sugar is the cookery-antidote to salt. Should you by accident make gravy or soup too salty, add a teaspoon of brown sugar and the briny taste will disappear.

❖

At a time when eggs are scarce and expensive, I found that by substituting an extra heaped tablespoon of butter for an egg, cakes were just as light and fluffy and seemed to keep moist longer.

When needing to boil milk, avoid burning it by boiling a tablespoon or two of water first. When water is boiling rapidly, add the milk; it won't burn and the saucepan will be easier to clean.

❖

To quickly melt butter, put it into a soup-ladle with a long handle and hold it over the flame.

❖

Egg yolks that have been separated from the whites and are not required for immediate use can be kept fresh by placing them in a cup and covering them with cold water.

❖

Place a clean jam-tin on the back of the fuel-stove, put into it a cup of water and 1/4 cup of sugar; cover and add daily a little water and a little sugar. In a few days the tin will be half-full of rich caramel. A spoonful colours and flavours meat dishes, gravies and soups, and two tablespoons added to boiled fruit puddings ekes out eggs. Good also as a caramel sauce over hot steamed puddings with custard.

❖

THE MILK TEST

You can test the purity of milk with a steel knitting needle; if the milk runs off the needle quickly, water has been added by your dairy farmer or the milkman. Pure milk will cling to the needle, dropping off slowly.

Glaze for pastry may be made without egg white. Mix a tablespoon of brown sugar with a tablespoon of milk; boil together and use when cold.

❖

If a boiled egg cracks in the water, you should crack the other end, too. The contents will then not be forced out.

Instead of making holes in the pastry of meat pies to allow steam to escape, or using egg-cup shaped steamers, simply insert two 'pipes' of macaroni into the pastry. This lets out the steam, but keeps in the gravy.

❖

Just before putting the crust on a steak and kidney pie, sprinkle with pepper and ground nutmeg.

Baking powder rolls are simple and easy to make: take 1 pound flour, 2 teaspoons baking powder, 1 small teaspoon salt, milk and water to mix. Sieve flour, baking powder and salt together, mix to dough with sufficient milk and water. Knead lightly, roll to 3/4 inch thickness and cut rounds with a scone cutter. Make each roll into a ball with your hands. Brush tops with milk and bake for 15 minutes in hot oven.

❖

Pawpaw scones are the flavour of the tropics. Peel, seed and chop a small ripe pawpaw, cook gently until soft and mushy. Do *not* add any water. Drain any excess liquid. Measure out a good 1/2 cup of pulp for every batch to be made. Cream 2 tablespoons of butter with 1/4 cup castor sugar, add a beaten egg and the pawpaw, mix well. Add 2 1/2 cups self-raising flour and 1 teaspoon salt alternately with 3/4 cup milk. Work until smooth dough is formed. Knead gently, cut into scone shapes and bake on a buttered tray for 12–15 minutes in hot oven. Brush top with melted butter mixed with nutmeg and cinnamon.

❖

Eggless scones, quick and easy. Sift 2 cups self-raising flour with 1 tablespoon sugar. Rub in 2 1/2 tablespoons of butter, add 3/4 cup of milk. Mix quickly, knead lightly, and bake in a hot oven. With a little more liquid added to make dropping consistency on to a griddle iron, this mixture makes a good drop scone.

Here is a good basic scone recipe: 1 pound self-raising flour, 2 ounces cooking butter, 1 level teaspoon salt, 11/2 cups of milk. Remember, a good hot oven is necessary to make good scones; quickness in the making is essential, and a damper mix rather than a dry mix will produce the goods. Glaze the top with milk, or make a thin paste of milk and icing sugar for sweet scones and glaze with this.

❖

Any fruit can be used in scones, but I like chopped dried apricots. Cover some dried apricots with barely a tablespoon of water and let stand before draining and adding as you make the scones.

❖

Do not cover scones with a heavy cloth just after taking them from the oven; too much steam rises and often causes the scones to become 'doughy'.

❖

When making fried scones, plunge each spoonful of the mixture into cold water before putting in the pan. This prevents the scones from absorbing the fat.

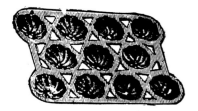  

This hint comes from a first-class chef. I took it and was delighted with the result. When baking scones leave the oven door slightly ajar until they rise, then close the door *gently*.

❖

Save all left-over quantities of jam, and place in a saucepan with a knob of butter and a beaten egg. Cook for 6 to 7 minutes. Makes an excellent filling for little tarts.

❖

For a delicious start to the day, slice pawpaw onto a glass dish, cover with the pulp or two or three passionfruit and squeezed orange juice. This gives you as much Vitamin C as you will need all day.

❖

Put a couple of sprigs of mint and a teaspoon of sugar into each glass and pour hot tea over. Very refreshing and tastes like mint julep without intoxicants.

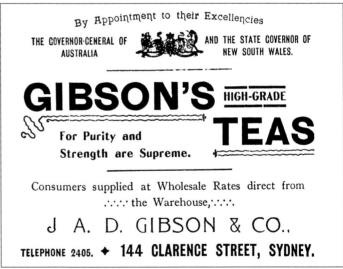

❖

Plain old iced coffee is always a winner. Place 1 cup very strong black coffee, 11/2 pints cold milk, 2 tablespoons sugar syrup and 2 serves vanilla ice cream into a large cocktail shaker, or a large screw-top jar and shake vigorously. Serve in tall glasses.

If hot milk is poured into a jug which is standing in cold water no skin will form on top of the milk.

❖

A good home-made cordial, a favourite with many families. Take the grated rind and juice of three large lemons and three large oranges, 1 ounce citric acid, 1 ounce tartaric acid, 1 packet (the old packet was about 2–3 ounces) Epsom salts, 6 cups sugar. Pour 10 cups boiling water over all this. Let stand for about 12 hours, then strain and bottle. Use as you would a cordial.

❖

A handful of salt thrown into the oven in which something has been burnt will at once prevent all unpleasant odour.

❖

When making a fruit-cake, dredge the fruit with a quantity of the baking-power to be used. Thus treated, the fruit will never sink to the bottom.

HOME-MADE DRY GINGER ALE

Peel two lemons, removing all the pith, and slice thin slices into a bowl with 1 pound sugar, 1/2 ounce cream of tartar and 1 ounce bruised root ginger. Pour over 5 quarts of boiling water and mix well. When cooled to blood-heat, stir in 1 ounce yeast. Cover with a cloth and set in a warm place for 24 hours. Skim and strain through a muslin cloth. Pour into bottles and cork down securely. You can also put into screw-top jars if available. Set aside for two days before using.

When a recipe calls for half a cup of butter, have a cup half-full of water and then drop in the butter until the water overflows. A sure measure!

❖

To make a sponge very light and high, beat the eggs with a little bicarb of soda before adding the sugar and beating in the usual manner.

When pouring sponge mixture into the tins, pour from a height, as the air gathered as it falls makes the finished sponge even-textured and feathery.

❖

When making a sponge cake and you only have very fresh eggs from the nest, cover them with cold water for 20 minutes before using. They beat up much quicker.

A prize-winner's tip: when you have the sponge mixture in the dish, give it a slight bump on the table. All the air bubbles disappear and a fine sponge results.

❖

When eggs are expensive make several kinds of cake at the same time; beat (say) three eggs and use 2 tablespoons of the beaten egg for each egg in the recipe. The cakes are just as good and the saving is considerable.

❖

A stale cake can be made to look and taste like a freshly baked one if it is put in a pudding-basin, then into a steamer, covered with a lid and steamed for half an hour. Good, too!

❖

If you find the top of a cake is cracked when removed from the oven, dampen a piece of old linen or thin tea-cloth in warm water, wring it out, and place it over the crack; this will soon bring the edges together.

❖

The popular 'meringue-and-marshmallow' cakes will rise to greater heights if baked on wet greaseproof paper on an oven tray instead of in a tin.

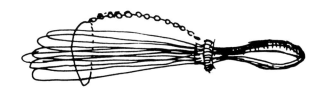

If a small piece of bread is put into the pan when frying fish it will prevent the fat from splattering, and also show by its colour when the fat is ready for the fish to be cooked.

If a cake sinks in the middle, put a dish of boiling water in the bottom of the oven and put the cake on the next shelf. This has been successful even after the cake has got cold.

No need to despair if your cake has 'sunk' in the middle! Place an enamel plate on the top of the cake tin, and turn the gas on full for five minutes. Then turn down the heat and bake for the required time. The cake will be a winner, and no one need suspect the possible failure.

To freshen stale cake, or small cakes that have been left in the oven too long, put a slice of fresh bread in the tin. The cakes draw the moisture from the bread; the bread becomes dry and hard, and can be used for breadcrumbs.

Marmalade is an excellent substitute for mixed candied peel in cakes. The firmer the marmalade the better.

Half a cup of milk in which a dessertspoon of brown sugar has been dissolved makes a splendid glaze for cakes, pastry, home-made bread and yeast buns, giving quite a professional touch.

TOPPINGS AND GLAZES

Instead of icing a cake, make a delicious crust by buttering the cake-top while hot and quickly sprinkling with cocoa (or cinnamon) and sugar.

❖

In case you are out of icing sugar, live many miles from your grocer and wish to make a cake, boil half a cup of sugar in a tablespoon of milk, add cocoa or a little vanilla and a little cochineal and spread it over the cake while it is still warm. Sprinkle a little coconut or chopped nuts over, and allow to set.

If stewing quinces, don't remove the seeds. Use plenty of sugar – about a cup of sugar to a cup of water – and let the quinces cook until they are a bright pink colour and the syrup jells. Drain, allowing the liquid to set for a delicious jelly. Use the fruit with custard.

❖

If quinces break badly when being cooked, mash them with a fork, add a tablespoon of honey and use as a tart filling, or put into small pastry shells.

If eggs are short, a tablespoon of golden syrup in a cup of warm milk equals three eggs. Golden syrup used in a pudding will serve the purpose of sugar; eggs and milk will keep it moist. A touch of bicarb of soda also helps when no eggs are available.

❖

Add a little salt (about 1/4 teaspoon to a pound) when stewing apples. Only the usual sprinkling of powdered sugar will then be required when serving.

❖

One finely grated carrot will equal one egg in a cake or pudding; add 1/4 teaspoon of bicarb soda also.

❖

In hot weather, if bothered with thin cream which won't turn to butter without endless stirring, dissolve half a junket tablet and stir it in to the cream. The cream will thicken in no time.

❖

When cooking turnips or cabbage, place a slice of bread on top of the water in which they are boiled. This prevents the smell from going all through the house.

Spectacles cleaned and polished with ordinary eau de Cologne will not smear when the wearer is cooking over the stove.

❖

To make a green tomato tart, slice full-grown – but not yet 'turning' – tomatoes, sprinkle well with sugar and add lemon juice. Put a layer of brown breadcrumbs on the bottom of the pastry before cooking in a moderately hot oven. Served cold with corned beef or other cold meats, it is nice for a change.

To prevent cooking odours from invading the rooms beyond the kitchen, fill a small fruit tin with vinegar and place it on the back of the stove.

❖

To make an economical 'baked' custard when eggs are scarce, bring a quart of milk to the boil. Mix a tablespoon of arrowroot, 2 tablespoons of sugar, half a cup of milk and a beaten egg. Put into a pudding dish and pour boiling milk over, stir till thick, then bake in the oven as usual, using a moderate heat.

❖

Instead of boiling custards, mix two egg yolks with a tablespoon of sugar and beat very well. Mix a heaped dessertspoon of arrowroot with a little cold milk, add to egg and sugar mixture, then pour 'really' boiling milk over this, stirring all the while. Cover for the first 5 minutes to allow the egg to absorb the heat, and custard is ready to use.

❖

Omit the raisins and sultanas when making a bread and butter pudding and spread the bread with blackcurrant jam.

❖

If all the bananas are green – too green to eat – put them in a strong brown paper bag in a dark cupboard for a few days to ripen.

These prize-winning pikelets are easy to make. Put into a bowl a level cup of flour, make a well in it, break in an egg, add a pinch of salt, a tablespoon of melted butter, milk to mix and beat well. Then add a good teaspoon of baking powder, mixing again. Cook on a hot greased griddle.

Type all important recipes onto small squares of calico and make them into a cloth book. Cloth recipes are much easier to handle in the kitchen and are everlasting.

Improve the flavour of a chocolate cake by mixing in a heaped tablespoon of strawberry jam with the eggs. The cake remains moist, too.

Stir into fresh cream 1/2 teaspoon cinnamon and 2 teaspoons of powdered sugar for a delightful flavour with apple pie.

The correct order in which to place the colours for a Rainbow Cake, counting from the bottom: dark cake, pink cake, white cake, or light cake on top. Prizes in cooking competitions have been lost through having the colours reversed. Those who enter these competitions could have the best cake, and lose through wrong assembly.

Make a nice easy dessert by washing half a pound of large dates, cover them with milk and simmer until all the milk is absorbed. Place on squares of pastry or shortbread biscuits and serve with cream or custard.

❖

Do you have Chinese gooseberries growing? If so, add them to your fruit salad, peeled and sliced, or eat them with bread and butter. For years I only made jam with them, now they are used as a dessert.

❖

For a delicious North Queensland pawpaw coconut pie, heat 2 tablespoons of butter, add 1 cup of sugar, chopped ginger, the juice of two lemons and a medium-ripe pawpaw, peeled and cubed. Cook slowly until just transparent – nearly cooked, but not squashy. Stir in 11/2 cups desiccated coconut and set aside. Make a shortcrust pastry, line a shallow pie dish and put a top on the pie, or make two open pies. Fill mixture into shell(s) and bake in a fairly hot oven for 30 minutes. If left open, trim with pastry strips. Delicious served warm or chilled.

❖

Make good, strong, handy shopping bags out of hessian. Make different sizes for different shopping needs. Use 1/4-inch rope for the handles and use oddments of wool to work pretty flowers, or the word SHOPPING on the front. Can be washed and will last for years.

❖

After the summer has set in and the Coolgardie safe has been in use for a while, it is liable to become musty. To sweeten it, hang a bag containing two handfuls of charcoal inside and renew the charcoal from time to time.

❖

When ripe lemons are needed and only green ones are available, pack the lemons into a case and add a ripe apple every now and then. Put the case in a dark room, and in four days some of the lemons will be yellow and juicy.

❖

A handful of horsehair made into a wad makes a good and economical pot-scraper. Put the pad out in the sun occasionally to air it and sweeten it up.

❖

This lemon delicious pudding must be the most delicious treat ever; it is the forerunner of the 'self-saucing' puddings you can buy today, but this home-made one is far, far better than the commercial packet variety in supermarkets. Grease a 31/2 to 4 cup fireproof pudding dish. Cream 11/2 ounces butter with 1/2 cup sugar and fold in 4 tablespoons of sifted self-raising flour, the grated rind of a lemon and the juice of the lemon. Beat 2 egg yolks and stir into 11/4 cups of milk. Stir this slowly into the butter and lemon mixture. Beat the egg whites to stiff peaks, stir a little into the butter mixture first, then fold the remainder in lightly. Pour at once into the prepared dish and bake in preheated (moderate) oven for about 35 minutes. Enjoy this delightful dessert!

At jam-making time, fill a few small peanut-butter or similar jars with jam. They are always acceptable gifts for patients in hospitals who enjoy that home-made taste. The small jar is also just enough to fill a jam sponge sandwich instead of opening a larger jar.

❖

Jam that has failed to jell can be put right by adding a pint of 'made' jelly crystals of the same colour and flavour to every 5 pounds of fruit. Boil for 15 minutes after adding jelly.

❖

Keep paraffin wax (for sealing preserves, etc.) in an old aluminium teapot. It's so handy to use when sealing jars. It eliminates waste and can be popped on the range and heated in a moment or two. When a bottle of preserves is opened, the wax can be returned to the teapot for future use.

JELLY

A junket tablet crushed and stirred into a jelly will help it set in half the time. This is a hint worth knowing!

❖

In case jelly won't set through some slight error in the making, add the juice of a lemon.

❖

Did you know that a pinch of bicarb of soda will, if added to a jelly, set it firmly in less than an hour?

If rusty knives are soaked in raw linseed oil for a few hours the rust can be wiped off and the knife polished in the usual way.

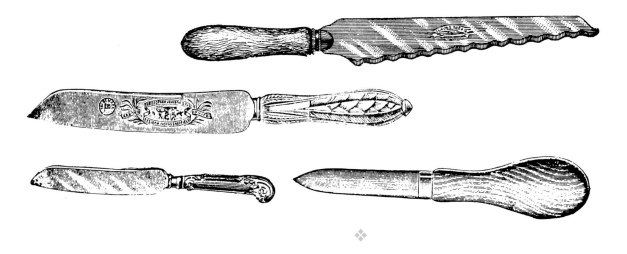

❖

Keep your lemon skins when squeezing the fruit and put them in the washing-up water with the dishes. The lemon will remove the grease and make the dishes sparkle.

Try new recipes in late autumn or winter. Chocolates, fondants and marshmallows are easiest to make in weather that is cool and dry. Home-made bread, buns, ginger or hop beer are better in the cool, but not the coldest, months; all kinds of jellies set well overnight without an ice-chest, puff or flaky pastry can be made only when the butter is firm, and potted meats, lemon cheese and boiled salad dressing, which can be made at any time, keep much longer in winter than they do in summer.

❖

Put a 'thin' bar or two of milk chocolate on each layer of a sponge sandwich as it comes out of the oven. As it melts, spread it smoothly over the cake, put layers together, melt and spread another bar over the top and sprinkle with finely chopped nuts. Different and delicious for Christmas parties.

Weigh, clean and chop all the fruit for a Christmas cake and weigh the butter, sugar, flour etc. the day before making the cake. Making it will not seem such a long process if prepared over two days.

❖

To make brandied cumquats, fill jars with crystallised cumquats, cover with brandy and allow to stand for two to three months. Put down by early October to use for Christmas.

❖

To make quick and easy pineapple chutney, peel, slice, core and chop 4 pounds of firm pineapple. Peel and chop very finely 6 cloves garlic, 2 large chillies and 4 ounces preserved ginger. Put pineapple and 1 quart vinegar into pan. Cook gently for half an hour. Add 1/2 pound brown sugar, 1 pound seeded raisins or sultanas, 1/2 teaspoon cayenne, 2 tablespoons of mustard seeds and 11/2 teaspoons salt. Boil gently for 11/2 hours or until thick. This chutney improves with age.

❖

Fish and tomato cups are tasty for luncheon. Put boneless fillets into ramekin dishes, sprinkle with pepper and salt and a little flour. Cover with brown breadcrumbs, a round of tomato and a dot of butter. Cook in oven for twenty minutes.

❖

Seafood pie can combine cooked flaked fish with the meat from crayfish legs and claws; add a small chopped onion, a dessertspoon of lemon juice, salt and pepper and a little white sauce. Top with mashed potato and bake.

❖

When frying fish, sprinkle the pan with a little curry powder – it not only stops the smell invading the house, but improves the flavour and colour.

❖

A NEW TOP FOR STEAK AND KIDNEY PIE

Into 1 cup of self-raising flour, rub 1 tablespoon of butter or good dripping. Mix in an egg to make moist. Flatten out the mixture with your hands and put on top of meat in the saucepan. No rolling! This turns out extremely light, and a change from baked pastry.

When eggs are scarce this is a good crisp batter for fish, or fruit such as apple and pineapple. Sift a half to a cup of self-raising flour, 1 level tablespoon of custard powder, salt and pepper and mix to a nice consistency with water. Dip fish fillets and fry in boiling fat.

❖

Dip cold meat pies in and out of cold water before reheating them and they will be crisp and juicy as when freshly cooked.

To make a nice dressing for crab or crayfish, remove the meat from the shellfish and keep the shells. Mix a little mustard with 1 tablespoon of vinegar, a small quantity of breadcrumbs, 1 tablespoon of thick cream and 1 teaspoon each of oil, salt and pepper; add chopped parsley. Return fish to shells and pour over the dressing. Serve with brown bread and butter and lemon wedges.

In the Laundry

❖

Washday was an arduous and regular undertaking in the days of our parents and grandparents. The copper was filled and lit, the laundry blue and starch prepared, and turning the mangle required a strong arm. Much heavy outdoor work resulted in clothes far dirtier than those most of us are used to today, and the style of life meant that tablecloths, doilies, and lace collars and cuffs were much in evidence – and they all found their way into the 'wash'.

When the whole family was assembled on the verandah for a portrait photograph, the gleaming whites and firmly starched frocks and trousers reveal the skill of the ordinary housewife. Dry cleaning and 'drip-dry, no-iron' fabrics were unheard of, and the women of the era were as accustomed to starching and dyeing as this generation is to automatic washing machines. The hints in this chapter give some idea of the time-consuming work undertaken in the laundries of the time, and provide some wonderful ideas still relevant today.

To retain the original stiffness of a 'voile' frock, add a teaspoon of sugar to the final rinsing water.

Dissolve an aspirin tablet in about 3 cups of water and soak your georgette blouse for a few minutes before rinsing through soap later. Removes perspiration marks wonderfully without having to rub.

During a tour of China and Japan we bought several sets of silk undies, beautiful to look at and delightful to wear. The merchants told us to give the garments their first wash in water containing one packet – about 2 ounces – of Epsom salts to a gallon of water. We followed instructions and the colours have remained unchanged.

When tinting white clothes any colour, mix a pinch of bicarb of soda in the hot water used for making the dye mixture. This makes the dye spread evenly and avoids patchiness and streaks.

Instead of scrubbing greasy overalls, place them in a bucket of warm water in which about 1/4 to 1/2 cup of Epsom salts has been dissolved; leave to soak overnight if possible, then wash in the ordinary way. It cuts the work in half.

To successfully clean a white imitation Panama hat, use white shoe-cleaner. Brush the hat free of dust, apply the cleaner sparingly on a fairly wet sponge and dry in the sun. Looks like new!

Legs of old pyjamas make excellent covers for the ironing board. They fit smoothly and are easily removed for washing.

❖

Instead of pulling out bones (or steel) which have pierced either end of corsets, press a piece of adhesive tape firmly over the hole. If necessary warm the tape before using.

❖

If an aspirin is added to the water when washing cretonnes the colours will not run and the fabric will be brightened.

Warner's
Rust-Proof

The addition of a teaspoon of olive oil to every gallon of water used for washing woollies will prevent them going hard and 'felted'.

Before washing mosquito nets, tie them loosely around the middle with tape. Don't untie the tape until the net is placed over the line. Much easier to handle this way.

Don't throw away an old hairbrush! Keep it in the laundry and use on the soiled parts of men's working clothes. Good also for soiled cuffs and collars. Saves a lot of rubbing.

❖

The old idea of dropping a lump of sugar into the teapot had this to commend it - the sugar will prevent linen from becoming stained if the tea is spilt on it.

❖

A tin of condensed milk boiled in the copper with the clothes on washday makes a lovely caramel filling for small tartlets; or, if thinned with a little hot milk, it makes a good pouring sauce.

❖

Small articles (such as hankies, table napkins and pillow cases) dried on a rosemary bush will retain the pleasing perfume when dry.

❖

When cracking almonds and walnuts, don't throw away the shells; a few handfuls wrapped in newspaper are very useful for lighting the wash copper, or the bath heater. They can be useful as kindling in the open fireplace as well.

Strip the cover from an old umbrella, enamel it white and hang it by the handle from a hook in the ceiling. This makes a capital drying rack cum airer, for it will hold a large quantity of small things. It takes up no space, is nicely out of the way, and can be closed up when not in use.

Your modern electric iron will stay smooth and shiny underneath if you soak a cloth in strong cold tea, and rub the iron with this. All stains will be removed.

❖

Even a bad scorch will usually yield to this technique. Saturate a piece of linen or muslin in peroxide and place over the damaged part. Press with a hot iron and the scorch will in most cases come off the cloth.

❖

To keep stored linens white, 'blue' an old pillow case to a deep blue and keep them in this.

❖

To make household linen smell sweet and fragrant, slip in among the folds a few 'aromatic' packets containing powdered cloves and lavender (1/4 ounce lavender flowers to 1/4 teaspoon of cloves).

❖

To remove the newness from new blankets, and make them beautifully soft, add 1/2 pound bicarb of soda to a tub of cold water and soak.

The very best way to hang sheets to catch all the wind is to peg one hem straight along the line, then bring up the other lower corners and peg these two-thirds of the way along the first hem. The sheet will balloon out with even the faintest breeze.

Lint, fluff or hair can be easily removed from woollen clothing by moistening a rubber sponge with water, squeezing it almost dry and applying it to the clothing.

If 'cut work' embroidery is ironed on the wrong side the pattern will stand out much better.

❖

When doing the washing, put 2 teaspoons of Epsom salts in the copper. No rubbing is required as the salts remove the dirt.

❖

Eggshells make an excellent bleach for clothes. Save all the shells in an oatmeal bag until washing day, then put the bag of shells into the copper with the clothes and boil.

❖

Keep the starch left over from the washing to put in the water used for washing the floor tiles; the colour of the tiles, especially dark ones, will be greatly enhanced.

❖

Keep dress-hangers handy on ironing day; the ironed frocks and shirts can be put away immediately to save time and creasing. If hubby is handy, ask him to put a hanging rail nearby.

❖

Before washing flimsy nets or laces, fold them into small shapes first and keep them thus through the laundering. This will save annoying tears.

To 'air off' an ironed collar quickly, fold it for a few moments round a jug filled with very hot water.

❖

When glace kid shoes have been scratched so badly that pieces of leather are raised up, apply a little egg-white to the torn pieces, press firmly down and polish as usual.

❖

To take a 'bag' out of a skirt, lay a heavy cloth over the part, damp well with a wet sponge and press with a hot iron, raising the iron and cloth each time to allow the steam to escape.

❖

A dried corncob from which the kernels have been removed will remove burrs and grass seed from clothing without injuring hands or material. Place the garments flat and use the corncob as a brush.

Household Cleaning

❖

Keeping houses of the time clean and in good order was a daunting task. Just as the housewife 'made do' in the kitchen by substitution and good use of leftovers, she 'made do' in the house by mixing her own cleaners and polishes and thinking up clever ways of making the results more lasting. Houses of the time were full of brass, silver and glass – all requiring constant care – and, of course, the open fires left smoke and dust on every surface.

The tips in this chapter relate to an era when leather chairs, rosewood pianos, crystal and silverware were in use. Other hints cover the more mundane elements of life: cleaning the copper for washday, or unclogging the kitchen sink. They all reflect the amount of time and effort that was required to clean the house, whether it was a grand residence or a simple cottage, in the days before vacuum cleaners and aerosol packs. They provide an insight, too, into the unremitting energy and dedication women brought to the task of keeping the family home spotless and fresh.

A kerosene tin to be used over the fire will be much easier to handle if two small handles are put on opposite sides, clothes-fashion, instead of over the top.

❖

When washing your best china and crystal, place a folded towel in the bottom of the sink or dish and another on the draining-board. This will save a lot of breakages.

❖

Glycerine well rubbed into leather chairs, etc., especially those used near the fire, will preserve the leather and help to prevent it from cracking.

❖

To clean rubber bath-mats, sprinkle with powdered borax, and rub well with a damp cloth until clean. Every trace of dirt vanishes.

❖

After polishing brass, rub it over with oil, thus stopping the action of the cleaning acid on the metal and protecting the surface from tarnishing too quickly.

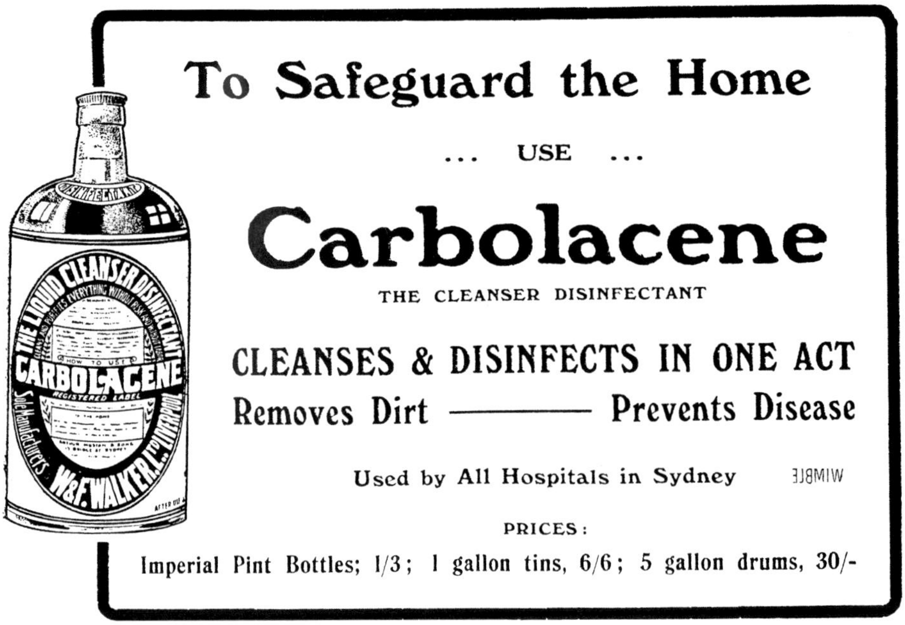

A handful of salt thrown onto the fire occasionally will keep the chimney clean and save the expense of a chimney sweep.

❖

A very easy way to clean diamond rings or brooches is to place them for a few minutes in half a cup of water with 2 teaspoons of bicarb of soda dissolved in it. Move about gently, and dry carefully with a soft cloth. Soap or other matter caught in the claw setting is removed this way, and the stones take on a new, fresh brilliance.

❖

To clean painted woodwork, mix baking soda (bicarb) to a thin paste with vinegar, then add a little salt. Rub painted work with a damp cloth dipped in the mixture. Wipe over with a clean damp cloth to dry.

❖

To clean sandshoes so that they will dry rapidly, use methylated spirits with the white cleaner instead of water.

❖

Polish crystal by rubbing with a soft cloth well moistened with methylated spirits; rub article well and dry with a soft cheese-cloth for that sparkling shine.

❖

Steam won't condense on the bathroom mirror if the glass is rubbed over with soap and polished with a dry cloth. This tip also applies to spectacles; handy when wearing them in a steamy atmosphere.

❖

Never polish an ebony or rosewood piano case with furniture polish, as it will probably crack the veneer. Use instead a few drops of kerosene sprinkled on a clean cloth.

Half a pound each of white sand, soft soap and whiting, and a cup of water make an excellent cleaner for sinks, baths and saucepans. Boil together until thick. (Like home-made sand soap!)

❖

If silverware is stored in powdered starch it will not tarnish and will not need polishing when taken out for use.

❖

If you run out of brass polish, mix fine ashes and kerosene to a paste and clean brass with it. It gives a good polish, and saves money.

❖

In the absence of oil, wet a cake of soap and apply to squeaking hinges; it acts instantly. Another good 'oiler' is hand cream.

❖

Mix equal parts of turpentine, olive oil and vinegar and keep in a clean bottle labelled 'Furniture Reviver'. Shake well before using. Apply as usual and polish with a soft, clean cloth. Good for walnut furniture.

❖

Make window-sash cords last three times as long as usual by rubbing them with soap. Treat only the few inches that are constantly passing over the pulley wheels.

❖

If the kitchen sink becomes clogged, drop 1 tablespoon of bicarb of soda down the pipe, pour in 1 tablespoon of vinegar and close up the pipe tightly. Leave for an hour or so, then flush thoroughly with water.

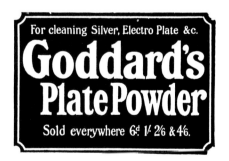

For cleaning Silver, Electro Plate &c.

Goddard's Plate Powder

Sold everywhere 6ᵈ 1⁄ 2⁄6 & 4⁄6.

❖

To protect furniture, leather upholstery and leather goods from mildew caused by sea air, use a polish made with equal parts of vinegar and olive oil. Shake well before applying, and polish with a soft, clean cloth. This mixture can be used on any kind of furniture and gives a good gloss. Keep in a corked bottle.

Blistering of paint on a front door exposed to the sun can be prevented by giving it a rub over once a week with olive oil. Polish with a soft cloth. Good also for any varnished hardwood doors.

❖

Liquid nail polish will securely cement broken glass – especially crystal – articles. Paint the edges, press together and hold firmly for a few minutes until the polish dries. Carefully wipe off any surplus.

❖

Dab a little face powder on your mirror and polish with a soft cloth for a good finish.

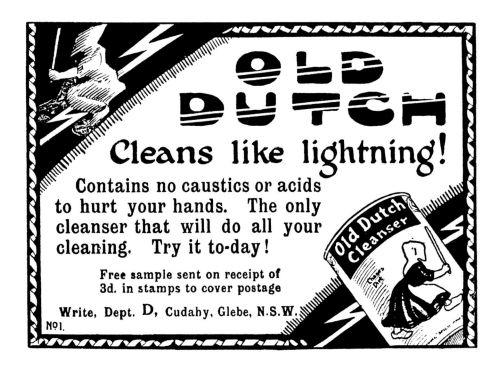

A very cheap oil-stain for wooden floors. Mix equal quantities of sump oil, kerosene, sheep dip and mineral turpentine – this last is cheaper than pure turps. This stain dries much more quickly, is darker, and lasts longer than raw oil and kerosene. The odour soon evaporates, leaving a good floor stain which gives good service.

To clean a pie dish when the contents have been burnt, dip it in very hot water, then quickly turn it upside down on a flat surface so that the steam cannot escape. The burnt portions will quickly come off.

Vinegar is excellent for removing smoke from woodwork and walls. Wet a cloth with vinegar and wipe over the surfaces; rinse with a soft, damp cloth.

If the tap is dripping, and a new washer is not available, turn the tap on full, put a few drops on oil on the stem, leave the tap running for a few more seconds, then turn it off. The dripping should cease.

To remove verdigris from the copper, mix a tablespoon of bicarb of soda with a tablespoon of kerosene. Scour the copper with the paste, rinse and dry.

❖

When running hot water from a gas heater into a porcelain bath, place an enamel plate or bowl just where the water falls into the bath. It is the first impact with the porcelain which imparts the green stain; as the water deepens the dish can be removed. This saves much cleaning to remove the unwanted stain on the bath.

Home Decorating

❖

Our parents and grandparents were just as keen to create comfortable and pleasant living environments as we are today, and they put their minds to the task with great inventiveness. This chapter reveals their clever use of cheap materials to achieve a desired effect and the simple techniques they employed to make the job easier. Lacking the financial resources to buy new, ready-made items, and with their menfolk busy at work for long hours, the women of the era turned to decorating through necessity and because they could see opportunities for improvement.

They were their own carpenters, painters, upholsterers and interior decorators, and were always on the lookout for ways of repairing or re-using items to hand. Often the budget did not stretch to employing tradesmen, and the ability of these women to tackle many jobs that most would not contemplate today is remarkable. Much was achieved using fresh paint, new coverings for furniture, and flowers for table centrepieces. The resourcefulness of these women, and their desire to create cheerful and comfortable homes, is reflected in the useful and practical tips in this chapter.

Instead of frosting a window, place mosquito netting over the glass and paint or whitewash on top of that. When dry, peel the netting off, and a very neat and pleasing effect is left – somewhat like stippling.

❖

Candles set in full-blown artificial roses and placed on a cork base make a charming table decoration. Clustered together in a float-bowl when there are no other lights in the room these 'rose candles' give a party a fairy-like effect to the table.

❖

When 'loose covers' are being made, boil the piping cord before using it in the cover. If left until the cover is washed, the cord will shrink and make the cover pucker.

❖

If you lack a long mirror in your bed-room, hang two small square ones at a lower height on the bedroom wall to reflect shoes and stockings.

❖

To mend decorative broken china, crush unslaked lime very finely and sift it through muslin. Rub the edges of the china with egg white, dust quickly with the lime and press pieces together. It will soon dry and the break will be imperceptible.

❖

Discarded, cracked gramophone records can have a second use. Place them in an oven until they become soft and pliable as putty. They can then be moulded into any fancy, useful shapes desired, by placing them on top of jelly moulds, basins, plates or the like. When set and hard again you can decorate them artistically with painted flowers or edge them with silver or gold paint, thus creating attractive ornaments for the house. The completed article has a rich ebony colour.

❖

To renovate shabby folding canvas chairs kept on the verandah, cover the faded canvas with floral cretonne and lacquer the chair to match your colours. Give your verandah a face-lift for Christmas, and the world will feel better all round.

Gay-coloured bath towels make attractive and comfortable cool cushion covers for the verandah chairs. Also bright in the sun-room, and so easy to launder.

❖

When tinting curtains, keep a little of the dye mixture in a bottle for later use. Each time you wash the curtains add a little of the mixture and they will not require re-tinting for some time.

❖

A cheap money box is useful for keeping used razor blades in. Enamel it to match the colour of your bathroom.

NAILS AND SCREWS

When a nail is needed for hanging a towel in the laundry or bathroom, drive the nail through a medium-sized cork before knocking it into the wall. This will prevent tears in the wall and rust marks forming.

❖

Before hammering a nail into the wall, immerse it in hot water until it is thoroughly heated and then drive it in. The plaster will not break or crack.

❖

Smear olive oil or petroleum jelly on a screw before putting it into any work; this helps both the 'putting in' and the 'taking out' and it prevents the screw from rusting.

❖

Nails that have been dipped in paraffin wax before being driven into a plastered wall will go in easily, hold more securely, and come out when pulled.

Hot vinegar and water will tighten seagrass chair-seats. Sponge well and leave out in the sun to dry.

❖

Before repapering the walls, cover all the grease spots with a good coat of shellac to prevent the grease marks from coming through the new wallpaper.

Bamboo tables, 'what-nots' and paper stands may now be old-fashioned, but if you have one, give it a coat of your favourite colour, and the result will be a piece of furniture easy to carry that will brighten any dull room, sun porch or weekend cottage verandah.

One 'bushwoman' I know stained all her floors in her home with bloodwood gum mixed with methylated spirits, the gum being found on trees growing close to her home. The stain was painted on, and when dry the floors were polished with beeswax from the bees' nests also on the property. The floors looked very nice, and she was saved the expense of buying linoleum.

When using candles for table decoration, remember this tip. If they are chilled for at least 24 hours in an ice-chest, they will burn only an inch an hour.

Enamel the handles of old curling tongs to match the colour-scheme of your kitchen and use them to remove hot lids from cooking utensils.

❖

To make fly-wire screens transparent from within while obstructing the view from without, paint the inside black and the outside white. The white surface reflects the light, thus increasing its value as a screen.

❖

Polished wooden picture-frames can be freshened by washing in clear warm water; gilt frames are best treated with a cloth wrung out in equal parts of water and methylated spirits.

❖

To quickly revive faded or drooping cut flowers, plunge the stalks into very hot water for a few minutes, take out, cut off the ends from the stalks and arrange in ice-cold water. Flowers treated thus will last twice the usual time.

❖

A sprig of mint placed in a vase among flowers forms an effective decoration and keeps the vases sweet and free from flies.

PAINTING AND PAPERING

Cayenne pepper mixed with the wallpaper paste will discourage mice, silverfish and other paper-eating pests.

❖

Hot vinegar will soften paint brushes that have become hard and dry. Soak them in the vinegar for a good hour or more, then wash in the usual way with hot soapy water. Hot vinegar will also remove paint stains from window glass. Apply with a flannel, then rub with a coarse cloth.

❖

To clean white paint, dissolve 2 tablespoons of powdered borax in a little boiling water and add enough cold water to make 3 pints. After dusting the paint work, sponge with this mixture. Rinse with tepid water and dry off with a soft cloth.

❖

When mending a hole in wallpaper, tear a patch large enough to more than cover the hole or tear. The torn edges will 'merge' with the rest of the paper much better than a cut edge.

❖

A paper picnic plate attached to the bottom of a paint tin while painting indoors will save a lot of drops from falling onto the lino or furniture.

When flowers are scarce and you need decoration, lacquer some wheat ears in bright colours. The effect is charming and decorative; they can be stored away and used again and again.

❖

ARRANGING SMALL FLOWERS

The easiest way to arrange pansies and tiny short-stemmed flowers is to melt down 2 dessertspoons of paraffin wax (from any chemist or grocer) and pour gently over the water in your container. It will solidify and form a thin cake. Pierce holes in this with a warmed thin knitting needle and insert the pansies, etc. to reach the water below.

To float heavy flowers on top of water in deep vessels, push a small pin through the bloom and into a cork which will float on the water. Artful decorations can be made this way.

❖

For a table centrepiece arrange short-stemmed flowers, such as pansies or phlox, in a bowl of wet sand covered with moss. This will not obscure the faces of guests as tall vases of blooms are inclined to do.

❖

If flowers are inclined to droop when first cut and put into water, leave them lying horizontally in cold water overnight; the stalks will stiffen and remain firm and upright for some time if treated this way.

❖

The water in which tulips are arranged should not be changed. Unlike other flowers, tulips last better in stale water. A little starch added to each vase stiffens the stems.

❖

UNPLEASANT ODOURS

The disagreeable odour emanating from some cut flowers even when the water is changed frequently can be neutralised if a small piece of charcoal is placed in the bottom of the vase. This won't affect the flowers. To completely dissipate the unpleasant smell from French marigolds, add about a dessertspoon of sugar to the water in the vase.

❖

Before doing any little painting jobs in the home, wipe the articles to be painted with a cloth dipped in turpentine. Besides completely removing any grease and dust, this helps the paint to dry quicker.

Making & Caring for Clothes

❖

Our mothers and grandmothers never sat empty-handed in the evenings or on Sundays. They knitted, crocheted and sewed, more often as a necessity rather than for recreation. Fancy layettes, including shawls, were created for new arrivals, and sturdy, hard-wearing socks and jumpers were knitted for the whole family.

Clothes and shoes were expensive items in those days, and were very carefully looked after. Often, garments worn for 'best' were donned just before an outing or event, and were removed and hung away as soon as the festivities were over. Ordinary weekday wear was protected by aprons and pinafores to avoid the too-frequent washing of clothes, and stockings were preserved in

good condition and mended again and again. Indeed all clothing was mended, repaired and re-used, handed down from child to child, and supplemented by creations cut down from garments worn out by adults. Everyday clothes were run up on the sewing machine as a matter of routine and in most households of the era, the reliable and durable treadle machine was in such frequent use that it occupied a place in good light in the sitting room.

For all the making of everyday overalls and socks, and the mending baskets that were never empty, these women still found time to turn their skills to decorative quilts and doileys and Sunday dresses for their little girls. The hints in this chapter reveal the variety of handiwork that these talented and capable women produced and give some idea of their dedication to the task of keeping their families 'neatly turned out'.

Fine needlework done in hot weather is liable to become soiled by contact with warm hands. To prevent this, rub the hands all over with powdered starch as often as necessary.

❖

To make stockings last longer, rub a piece of paraffin wax over the feet of the stockings on the inner sides, paying particular attention to heels and toes. Do this quite frequently. The wax leaves a deposit which reduces friction and thus helps to preserve the material. Silk, wool and cotton can be made holeproof in the same way.

❖

Sew buttons on your husband's clothes with posy wire. Using the wire as a needle, sew through several times and finish with a neat twist. There won't be any more buttonless garments!

Soak new stockings in a bowl of warm water with 1 table-spoon of salt dissolved in it. Next day, squeeze and hang to dry. During wear they will not ladder.

An excellent cover for protecting dresses hanging in outback wardrobes from dust can be made from an old pillow case. Unpick the centre of the stitched end a sufficient amount to insert the hook of the hanger, and pull the pillow case over the dress.

❖

Small tobacco cigarette tins with hinged lids kept in the sewing-machine drawer come in handy for pins, needles and loose buttons.

❖

Keep a small square of soap near your machine in lieu of a pin-cushion in which to keep your pins and needles. They will never go rusty again.

❖

When knitting a sleeve, or a 'V' neck in a garment, snap a press-fastener through every decrease row as you knit it. The number of decreases can be seen at a glance. The fasteners can be used again and again as the work proceeds.

If fingers are inclined to get hard and stiff with too much sewing and knitting, and many of us have this problem, keep a bowl of fine oatmeal and boracic powder handy and rub the hands into this mixture. Pamper your hands; oil them and powder them; they are the greatest machine a woman has, producing all kinds of miracles which most people take for granted.

❖

LASTING DARNS
Socks which have a great deal of heavy wear – farming folks – can be saved frequent mending if the wool to be used to darn them is first toughened by soaking it overnight in strong stale tea. Tannin toughens the strands and makes the darns last twice as long.

Snap fasteners may be sewn on quite accurately without bother if you sew them on one side first, then rub them well with chalk and press on the other side of the material. The chalk mark left behind shows the correct position.

❖

Fresh orange peel is excellent for restoring black shoes that have lost their smartness. Rub well with the inside of the rind, and then polish with a soft cloth.

❖

When cutting out patches for a patch-work quilt, use a piece of sandpaper for the pattern shapes and the cloth will not slip. The rougher the paper the better it clings.

❖

Keep a roll of surgical bandage in your sewing basket. It is handy for facing when letting out children's dresses, for slipping between front and facing of a fine dress to give extra strength, for tacking over holes in household linens. It has many uses and gives a good foundation for darning.

❖

When commencing to crochet a cap, use a steel hook, rather thick, instead of a bone hook. The cap will be much firmer and less likely to finish in a peak at the top after it has been worn a few times.

❖

LONG-WEARING STOCKINGS

A good tip for nurses. Service-weight stockings will last much longer if rinsed in methylated spirits.

HARD-WEARING SOCKS

To make extra-strong heels on men's and children's stocks, slip one, knit one for the whole of the plain row, and next row purl as usual. This makes the heel thicker.

❖

When knitting men's socks, knit a fine thread of silk or mercerised cotton into heels and toes. They will wear twice as long.

Unwanted artificial posies can be cleaned, pressed and used for appliqué work on cushion covers, tea cosies or table runners. They can also be worked onto a plain blouse.

❖

When making net-covers for milk jugs or basins, leave a small hem all round and run a length of round elastic through this, adding only a few beads at each corner. This cover will not blow off and is flyproof.

❖

When necessary to sew with a double thread, knot both ends separately instead of together. This prevents the cotton from twisting or tangling.

❖

A hint for dressmakers. If you have sloping shoulders, set the shoulder seams of your garment well back, as it gives a much 'squarer' line.

The New Tailored Gowns

Woollen suit with bone buttons.   Corduroy or velveteen suit with odd white silk revers.   Twilled woollen suit with facings, buttons, and hoops of satin.

Health & Beauty

❖

Country women of the era were out in all weathers, helping with haymaking, lambing and the like, and even women in the towns were involved in outdoor work such as taking care of poultry and filling the woodbox for the slow combustion stove and the chip heater. Keeping the skin of the face, neck and hands smooth and beautiful under those circumstances was something of a personal challenge, as the hints in this chapter reveal, and one seemingly shared by Australian women of every generation.

Even before the days of inexpensive cosmetics, much emphasis was placed on healthy, lustrous hair, well manicured fingernails, and soft, smooth skin. These resourceful women made good use of a variety of ordinary household items in their quest for health and beauty. Lemon juice, egg white and oatmeal were used for myriad purposes. Rosemary and other herbs from the kitchen garden were made into beneficial rinses and lotions.

Childhood illnesses and minor injuries were usually treated at home in those days. The humble Epsom salts had many uses, and no household was complete without a supply of bicarbonate of soda. Its many first-aid applications were of immense use

to country women who were mothers of large families and many miles from the doctor. Their wise and practical tips remain as useful today as then.

One teaspoon of sugar mixed with a small quantity of olive oil and rubbed well into the hands will remove stains and soften the hands nicely.

❖

When you come in from a hot tennis court, or from a hike, massage your feet briskly with ice-cold eau de Cologne. This refreshes your entire body.

❖

Every housewife knows the value of soaking the feet in Epsom salts. It is equally good for smoothing fingertips roughened by housework, and also improves the texture of the skin.

❖

In cases of arthritis, gently massage the joints with lemon juice and olive oil. This is of most benefit when the patient has been made warm.

❖

Your skin will acquire satin smoothness and your spirits will revive in a bath to which the juice of four lemons has been added. Then cleanse your face and throat and treat yourself to an oatmeal pack. Relax until the pack dries, then remove with cold water and treat the skin with lemon ice. To make lemon ice, mix two parts fresh lemon juice with one part water. Freeze into cubes.

FACE PACKS

Fine oatmeal makes a very good face pack. Mix a little with water, and after washing the face, smooth the paste over the entire face and neck. Use once a week for dry skins; twice if the skin tends to oiliness. Relax for 10 to 15 minutes while the pack sets, resting yourself as well as the face muscles.

❖

Another good face pack for early wrinkles is egg white. After cooking with eggs, smooth the residue left in the shells all over the face and throat. Quickly you will feel the skin begin to tighten. Give yourself a little rest while the pack does its work. Later, rinse off with warm water and apply a little vanishing cream.

If hair has begun to turn grey, it may be darkened to its original colour by the use of sage leaves. Simmer a handful of sage leaves in a saucepan with about 2 cups of water for about 20 minutes. Strain the mixture. When cold, brush it daily into the hair until the greyness disappears.

❖

Use an oil can which can be bought for very little money for applying oil, or hair lotion, to the scalp. This is more efficient and thus less wasteful.

❖

An ordinary card table makes an excellent bed-table for a sick child. Rest two legs on the floor, fold the other two up and the table fits right over the bed, providing the young patient with scope for his activities while confined.

❖

To make a non-sticky lotion for whitening and softening the hands, soak 2 tablespoons of oatmeal in a cup of water, leave overnight. Next day, strain the mixture and add the juice of a large lemon, 2 dessertspoons of glycerine and a little perfume. Store in a small bottle. Rub into the hands after washing up.

❖

Scrub elbows with warm soapy water and if necessary use a pumice stone; 'lean' the elbows in the two halves of a cut lemon for a few minutes daily.

❖

HOME-MADE BATH TONIC

I watched a woman gathering pine needles from beneath a large pine tree in the street near her home. 'There's nothing like a good pine needle bath after a tiring day,' she said. She told me that she boiled a handful of pine needles for about 20 minutes in a pint of water and then strained the liquid and added it to the bath. I tried it after a tiring day's shopping and found it very refreshing. Pine needles are easy to gather and cost nothing. You are just making use of something nature has given up.

A little lemon juice added to rosewater makes an excellent skin astringent.

❖

BLEMISH REMEDY

This is an old remedy to clear the skin. After washing the skin well, slice 4 lemons, add a dessertspoon of Epsom salts, a dessertspoon of cream of tartar, sugar to taste and 1 pint of boiling water. Stir well and leave to cool. Drink a wine glass of the mixture every morning before breakfast.

❖

To correct enlarged pores, rub a little pure alcohol diluted with an equal part of water into the skin at night.

❖

Your fingernails will take polish much better if first cleaned with lemon juice. Dip your orange stick in water to which lemon juice has been added.

❖

A few drops of rosewater added occasionally to a jar of face-cream will prevent the cream from drying out during dry weather. It will make it spread more evenly and 'go' further, saving the expense of another jar.

Dissolve 1/4 pound starch in a little hot water, add 1/2 cup of milk, stir together and add to bath water. This starch bath not only helps remove fatigue but is also smoothing to tender or sensitive skins and is a beautifier.

Mix equal parts of lemon juice and olive oil and rub on the fingernails. Polish with a soft pad. It leaves a rosy glow to the fingernails which lasts for days, and keeps the nails in good condition.

For dry hair, mix avocado and apricot oil together and work into the scalp. Work in circles from front to back, then back again. Leave on for half an hour before shampooing.

SHAMPOO FOR NORMAL HAIR

Brush your hair with mostly upward strokes for 5 minutes, then scrub, especially around the forehead, with a well-lathered nail brush, and massage the scalp well with the fingers. Rinse hair in clean warm water; then rinse in warm water to which the strained juice of two lemons has been added. Finally, rinse in clear cold water. A series of such treatments at intervals of ten days will endow your hair with beauty, life and sheen, freeing it from dandruff and scalp disorders. The acid of the lemon will strip the hair of 'soap curd' and the secretions of perspiration, and oil and alkali deposits.

From the best part of an old towel, make a pair of large mitts — no need to form a thumb. After washing your hair you can dry it very quickly with these. Make a pair of very fluffy mitts from a baby towel for quickly patting dry a baby or young child.

To make lemon hand lotion, mix two parts fresh lemon juice, one part glycerine, one part rubbing alcohol, perfume as desired. Use often, but especially at night.

A 'reviver' for tired-looking hair is simply to beat an egg yolk and rub it through the hair. Put on a shower cap, and allow 10 to 15 minutes for the reviver to take effect. Shampoo and rinse as usual.

❖

ROSEMARY FOR RESTORATION

Brunettes, before washing your hair boil up a handful or two of freshly picked rosemary leaves in 2 cups of water. Boil until it is reduced to about half a cup, and has turned dark-ish. Strain. When cool, rub this rinse into washed and dried hair. Keeping rubbing until the hair is dry again. This makes the driest hair soft and silky, stimulates the scalp, pre-serves and restores lost colour and leaves no sticky after-effects. Don't bottle it – use the rinse fresh.

The Men

While women's work of the time was mostly centred on home and family, men were out in the paddocks, on their 'round', or working in the shop, factory or office. Men worked hard to support families that were often large, and they in turn were given much care and support. Their capable women drew on a fund of practical knowledge to help them make the life of the breadwinner more comfortable, both at work and at home. Ideas here range from providing easily prepared food for bush trips to ways of keeping the tobacco moist for Dad's after-dinner pipe on the verandah.

Although the ordinary husband and father had few recreational hours, women exercised great inventiveness in turning inexpensive items to good use for fishing, shooting and camping outings. They also devoted much thought to providing nourishing and appetising food before, during and after the working day, and even had hangover remedies in their repertoire. Much time was spent in conserving and extending the life of shoes and clothes, and they employed ingenious methods to keep their men warm, dry and clean.

Many hints in this chapter reveal the depth of concern and the nurturing qualities of the women, often expressed in small but significant ways. They convey an impression of partnership and unity of purpose that enriched the lives of the whole family.

Blunt razor blades can be more quickly sharpened if the strop is moistened with a little sweet oil and then sprinkled with a little flour of emery. Rub the resulting paste in well, then strop in the usual way.

❖

Chopped raisins and horseradish make a good relish to serve with meat, hot or cold. Men love it.

❖

Don't go into the scrub cutting or snigging without taking a tin of 'cocky's joy' with you. Besides being a good spread on dry bread, it's reviving in the pannikin.

For men working out in the open in very cold weather, the legs of old woollen socks make warm, cosy mittens. Cut off the foot, stitch around cut edge to make firm, cut a hole for the thumb and button-hole around this. These mittens keep hands warm on the coldest days and have cost you nothing but time.

Large tins, such as those for preserved fruit or jam, make good bait tins for your husband. Neaten the edges and attach a wire handle. They also make useful emergency billies or saucepans when out camping.

❖

Make a handy bag for fishing tackle – or cartridges if your husband goes shooting rabbits – by cutting to a larger size an old football cover. Attach a strap of the right length to fit over the shoulder.

❖

Keep tobacco moist during winds or cold weather by putting a thick fresh orange skin into the jar.

❖

Keep old toothbrushes handy in the farm workshop or engine-room. Dipped in kerosene they will brush away oil and dirt accumulations from engine parts difficult to clean with a rag.

❖

When making the pot of tea at dinner, fill a thermos flask and leave it for those working late on the farm. Very tired, late workers appreciate that cup of tea put straight into their hands when they come in the door.

❖

If the men are going out into the bush, make a hearty round of scones by adding half cup of fine oatmeal to the ordinary mixture. A little more milk may be needed. They can toast them over the camp-fire if they like.

DAMPER

Soften one tablespoon of butter, or half butter and half clarified dripping, rub into 2 good cups of self-raising flour, add a good 1/2-teaspoon salt and an almost full cup of milk. Mix quickly and cook in a hot oven.

Before he starts out on a day's milk or butcher's run give your husband a bottle of hot soapy water wrapped in an old clean towel. He will find it comes in handy, and the water keeps warm for hours.

❖

Fill wet boots with dry oats and set aside for a few hours. The oats will draw out the moisture and prevent the leather from shrinking and cracking. Dry out the oats and use again. When they are no longer needed, feed the oats to the fowls or the horses.

To soften the hands after working with cement all day, wet the hands in warm water, sprinkle with sugar and rub in until the oil in the sugar begins to appear. Keep working around the nails, then rinse off with warm water and dry thoroughly.

❖

A 'PICK-ME-UP'

Cut the firm pulp of half a ripe pawpaw into small dice and place in tall glasses. In a jug, mix the juice of 2 lemons, 1/2 cup tomato juice, a teaspoon Worcestershire sauce and a pinch of cayenne. Pour the mixture over paw-paw in each glass and top with cracked ice. A dash of rum may help those in need of a 'hair of the dog'.

If in the bush rounding up cattle, or on the trail camping out, an efficient pot-scraper can be made by tying a handful of green blackboy (grass tree) tops together. It penetrates into corners even mitts can't reach, is wonderful in removing burnt food and is easily replaced.

Old bushmen used to pack septic sores with salt to aid the healing, but this is a painful process that probably only stalwart old-timers could endure. Bathing sores with salt and water is, however, very beneficial, and a foment made of boiling saline and a cloth placed over the sore is an excellent dressing. You can heal many sores yourself with careful washing and dressing with a saline pack.

The best portions of a worn 'honeycomb' quilt cut and neatly hemmed make excellent roller-towels for the men as they wash after a day's work.

Carbon tetrachloride, used on all sheep stations for drenching sheep, is an effective and rapid remover of obstinate stains – particularly greasy ones – from all clothing. Good for men's suits and not as dangerous as petrol.

Dust has taught outbackers this use for cellophane. A watch or clock can be well protected from the all-pervading dust by being encased completely in a neat transparent envelope. For pocket and wrist watches in dusty cattleyards and the like, the transparent wrapper from a cigarette packet is a handy and convenient substitute.

❖

Screw several cup hooks into the sides of the step ladder, so that many items such as paint pots, brushes, buckets and other cleaning aids can be hung there for convenience; surprisingly handy.

❖

This is a water-resisting glue, good for many outside jobs. Boil 2 pounds of the best glue in 2 quarts of skim milk, stirring well. Use as any other glue.

❖

The old bush hat with the row of corks is a good way to keep off flies, but if each cork is dipped in a little phenyl and allowed to dry before being attached to the hat, it will work twice as well.

❖

If your menfolk are out in all weathers, have an extra pair of thick soles attached to the bottom of their boots. Don't let the boots wear down to the original soles as the uppers are always good when the sole wears out. And no more wet feet!

Make a quick, handy mask from a man's large handkerchief. Fold form corner to corner 'V' shaped, tie a knot at both corners and attach a thick rubber band within the knot. This is easy to slip over the nose and mouth when doing dusty jobs.

❖

No matter how tired the men are after a very hard day's work on the farm, I generally hear them laughing and chatting pleasantly as they wash themselves before dinner. Where the wash-towels hang, in what was the dullest section of the built-in verandah, I have made a little 'art gallery' of humorous pictures and inspiring poems, quotations and jokes. From time to time I change them, putting the best into a scrapbook to look at in years to come.

❖

If you are working in the open and flies are very troublesome, tie a handkerchief smelling of lysol round your neck. This will keep them at bay.

BEER BREAD

This bread doesn't need yeast; it is supplied by the beer. Take 11/2 to 2 pounds of self-raising flour, half a bottle of beer, and about 2 level teaspoons of salt and sugar. Mix together and let stand for a while to 'prove'. Cook in a round tin if at home, or in a camp oven if in the bush.

An old bush tip which still holds good: soak lamp-wicks in vinegar for a few minutes before use. This prevents the lamps from smoking.

❖

Before wearing new boots or shoes, mix and melt over a slow fire 1/2 pint drying oil, 1 ounce yellow wax, 1 ounce turpentine and 1/4 ounce Burgundy pitch. Apply with a sponge to make footwear waterproof.

❖

A paste made by mixing oatmeal with kerosene will remove all stains from the hands. A good 'degreaser' as well.

❖

TO CLEAN WINDSCREENS

To clean windscreens so that rain will run off the glass, mix 8 tablespoons glycerine with 1 teaspoon of salt and 2 tablespoons of water. Apply very sparingly with a soft rag. This is also good for the outside of windows. The mixture repels the rain, allowing clear vision in wet weather.

❖

Vinegar is good for loosening rusty nuts, bolts and screws. The acid eats into the rust, making the job easier.

❖

Out of Doors

❖

These were the days when cows, poultry and horses, as well as household pets, formed an integral part of the life and livelihood of the family. In the fowl yard a broody hen was 'set' on a dozen eggs, hatching out a brood that provided the family with a constant supply of good fresh eggs. The cow grazed in the side paddock and every morning gave her wholesome milk. The horses that worked in the paddocks provided the children with mounts for school and, hitched to the buggy, became the transport to town – all this as well as taking part in the local show.

Such rich and rewarding resources in turn required good care and careful husbanding. All the animals belonging to a household needed to be warmly housed and well fed. They had to be kept in a sound, healthy and comfortable condition which often required skilled nursing through a number of common ailments. Protective measures were needed against pests, predators, accidents and illness whose range and diversity would daunt many modern housewives. Unwanted creatures such as flies, rats and mice, fleas and other vermin had also to be dealt with. Simple chemical-free remedies that posed little or no threat to the environment were used; all of these are perfectly applicable today.

The hints in this chapter reveal the busy routine and the trials and complexities, that our mothers and grandmothers faced so cheerfully in their care and nurture of the wide variety of animals for which they were responsible.

Our old fighting rooster had his style cramped when we cut two pieces of rubber tubing – slightly longer than his spurs – and fitted one on to each spur. They may have hurt his pride, but they proved most effective.

❖

When making or buying a new kennel for the pet dog, make certain the roof is hinged or detachable. You will then be able to air and keep the kennel sweet and clean with greater ease.

❖

If stray cats are trying to get at cage-birds or chickens in a coop at night, place a few sheets of sticky fly-paper around the cage or coop. It doesn't hurt the cat, but gives him so much trouble he won't come back.

❖

To completely banish cockroaches, mix boracic acid with boiled, mashed potatoes – about half and half. Roll the mixture into balls and place in the cockroaches' haunts. Be sure these balls are out of the reach of children.

Save all your vegetable peelings and boil them up every morning. Mixed with the pollard and bran for the fowls, it provides a good breakfast for them, and the return in eggs to you is worth the effort.

❖

When poddying lambs, don't add any water to the milk; add cream and warm it in a pot; cow's milk isn't as rich as ewe's. For weak lambs, a small teaspoon of brandy in a little warm milk is a big help. Feeding by the bottle is the best way, as each gets its share; in feeding by basin the biggest tends to get the most.

❖

When our clucky hen, Biddy, was bitten by a snake two days after her clutch had hatched out, I cut an old cardboard hatbox to a suitable size and tied a moulting feather boa to the top of the box, letting the loops hang down for the chicks to nestle under. All the chicks survived.

❖

Ducklings fed on well-boiled wheat will be ready for market – and delicious – at three months.

If compelled to doctor a cat, place the animal in a man's old coat sleeve. Hold the cuff firmly round its neck and tie the other end. This hint saves a great deal of drama for all parties.

Faintly colour the drinking water of young ducks with Condy's crystals – one grain to one quart of water – and the ducklings will remain healthy and free from snuffles.

❖

The health and vigour of cage-birds will be much improved if a teaspoon of lime is added to each gallon of drinking water thrice weekly.

❖

When the best cow in the yard became very weak, and food and milk were scarce, we thought we would lose her. It would have been a sad day for the whole farm; she was a real pet. Unbeknownst to us, Mother was sneaking her a pint of milk a day to feed her. In a sarcastic mood, my sister said 'Eggs are plentiful; why not give her an eggflip a day?' Mother tried the idea and soon our six-year-old Strawberry was skipping around like a two-year-old.

If garden gates around the farmhouse are hung to swing out-
wards, there will be much less danger of straying stock forcing an
entrance, causing you annoyance and frustration in having your
garden trampled. Allow for the fact that, though very intelligent,
animals will be animals, and if they see luscious feed, they will
want to eat it.

❖

Here are several successful ways to get rid of silverfish. Paint all
chinks, cracks and crevices in cupboards and drawers with
benzoline; put pyrethum powder, sampholine or whole cloves in
boxes where furs and clothing are stored; fill small bags of
calico with black pepper.

❖

As most liniments and stock drenches contain volatile spirits,
do not use them near an open fire.

❖

Rabbit or 'possum skins which have been alum-tanned will not
split when sewn if they are well rubbed with linseed or castor oil
as soon as the curing is complete.

Bee-keepers should provide facilities for the bees to get water without effort or danger of drowning. Keep fresh water in a bucket or other vessel and put a thick layer of ground cork on the surface of the water. Change the water often to keep the cork fresh.

❖

To prevent flies from gathering in a manure pit, sprinkle a quantity of borax over the manure. Using a fine sieve, scatter some more borax around the outer edges, then sprinkle water over the entire surface. Borax does not affect the fertilising properties of the manure.

❖

EPSOM SALTS

As a purgative drench for cattle and sheep, for cattle, one and a half cups in a tub of water; for sheep, half a cup in a tub of water. As a flush for poultry from a third to half a cup in three to four gallons of water. Do not feed until liquid is consumed.

There will be no danger of losing a saddlecloth if two narrow strips of strong material are sewn across the outer sides so that the inner saddleflap can slip through them.

❖

Sulphur added to chicken food will rid the birds of external parasites.

❖

A good 'foster mother' for orphaned chicks can be made by cutting woollen socks into strips and tacking them to the inside top of a packing case so that they just clear the ground. The chicks run in and out at will and need attention only at feeding time. I have saved many a clutch like this.

One infallible guide in culling poultry: the first ones to go to roost are the 'drones'.

❖

There is no need to buy expensive horse blankets for 'Dobbin', but do keep him warm on those frosty nights if he is the working pet on the farm. Make him a double hessian blanket, bound with strong black tape, and print his name on the side in the same black tape. Sew your name and address on the inside just in case he wanders off too far.

A clump of bamboo grown in the chooks' yard will supply green shoots at the height of summer. When the dry leaves fall they supply scratchings, especially in a large clump. The clump provides a welcome shade and helps to camouflage any unsightly fowlhouses. The clump also provides a good nesting place for a broody hen, and young turkeys greatly relish the young bamboo shoots.

❖

Did you know that first-year ganders are unreliable breeders?

❖

Change from wheat to barley for your hens if more 'cluckies' are required. Even white leghorns will respond to the change.

❖

A white line about one inch thick painted on the footpath around a building will discourage the attention of dogs. Paint the line about six inches from the wall. It works in most cases.

FLEAS

A little sulphur added to the dog's drinking water will help discourage fleas from the animal's coat.

❖

To rid a dog of fleas, boil a quantity of mint in a quart of water and strain. After washing and rinsing the dog as usual, pour the cooled mint water over his coat and allow to dry naturally. The dog loves it and the fleas depart quickly.

❖

Put half a cup of vinegar in the rinsing water after washing Fido; this chases fleas out of his coat and doesn't worry him like some flea powders do.

❖

To banish fleas from under a house or a shed where a dog has been sleeping, throw some salt about on the affected area. This is a cheap and effective remedy.

Several button-reflectors attached to a dog's collar will reflect a car's headlights after dark and give most drivers time to slow down to avoid hitting the animal. The reflectors used on bicycles are suitable for the purpose.

❖

Instead of sweeping the fowl-run every few days, loosen the soil and sprinkle the ashes from the stove over the loosened ground. This not only makes a good dustbed for the fowls, but a few shovels of this soil makes good manure for the garden when you decide to have a clean-out.

❖

A last word about fowls. Don't give apples to your poultry. Poultry-farmers find their hens go off the lay directly they have been given apples to eat.

❖

To keep stray dogs at bay, mix horseradish, vinegar and cloudy ammonia together. Let it stand in the sun for a few days before putting it near the haunts of the troublesome animals.

❖

Piglets reared away from their mother can be easily induced to drink milk if it is put in a shallow tin and their front trotters placed in the milk. As soon as they feel the milk on their feet, they drink readily.

❖

If a horse which is usually quiet begins suddenly to rear and plunge without apparent reason, examine his legs, rump and under his throat for the yellow eggs of the bot-fly and the fly itself. Kerosene dabbed on the eggs will kill them.

❖

MICE

A rat or mice bait that never fails: put a small piece of bread sprinkled with plenty of coconut on the trap. The coconut draws them every time.

❖

Fill tiny mouse-holes in the skirting-board with soap or make another hole near the first one for the soap. Mice hate it and will not come near.

To prevent scour in young calves, add a teaspoon of bicarb of soda to their morning milk about three times a week until they are a month old.

❖

To scare cats away from garden beds, get some bottles, place a few drops of ammonia in each and bury them up to their necks in various places. Renew the ammonia as necessary. This prevents other people's pets becoming your pests.

❖

To cure sores on a cow's teat, mix a tablespoon of eucalyptus oil with two dessertspoons of Vaseline or saltless dripping and apply after each milking. Six applications should clear up the most stubborn case.

To stop a cow putting its head through the fence, tie a stick behind its horns. The stick should protrude about a foot on either side of its head. It will soon learn to keep away.

ANTS

A lemon cut in halves and placed where small ants are troublesome will usually rid the place of them, and often works with larger ants, too. Alternatively, dust shelves and cupboards thoroughly with ground cloves.

FLIES AND INSECTS

Make a 'decoy' for flies by sprinkling a few currants onto sticky fly-papers. A few grains of sugar here and there on the paper attracts them also. Papers should be burnt frequently.

❖

Don't let flying insects keep you from sitting under your favourite tree. Fill an empty sauce bottle with a little vinegar-water that has been sweetened with sugar. Tie the uncorked bottle to an inconspicuous branch, and see how many are attracted to it.

❖

To prevent flies settling on electric-light bulbs, lampshades and other fittings, sprinkle the fittings with a little camphorated oil.

❖

To clear a room of flies, fill a large basin with boiling water, then add a dozen drops of lavender oil. Flies and insects dislike it, but the fragrance is pleasant in the room.

Time Off

❖

The limited time available for recreation in this era was spent in a variety of ways. In town, tennis parties and cricket matches were becoming popular; in the country, the family picnic or bush trip was a popular source of pleasure. Great preparations were made for these outings: the hampers packed full of delicious, home-made provisions, the billy stowed carefully into a saddle-bag or cart, suitable hats and boots donned, and the horses saddled.

Some lucky folk took holidays to the seaside or other parts of the country, and a few even packed their trunks for long sea voyages to other parts of the world. Most, however, contented them-

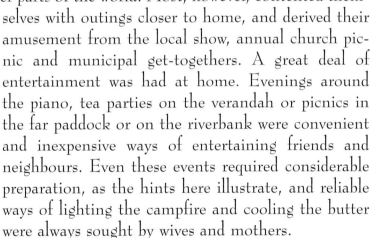

selves with outings closer to home, and derived their amusement from the local show, annual church picnic and municipal get-togethers. A great deal of entertainment was had at home. Evenings around the piano, tea parties on the verandah or picnics in the far paddock or on the riverbank were convenient and inexpensive ways of entertaining friends and neighbours. Even these events required considerable preparation, as the hints here illustrate, and reliable ways of lighting the campfire and cooling the butter were always sought by wives and mothers.

Our mothers and grandmothers were expert in planning and preparing for these family-centred forms of relaxation. The hints in this chapter reveal that no detail was overlooked, and that their economical and practical ideas contributed greatly to the enjoyment of the whole family.

Carry a square of waterproof canvas or sailcloth in the car for laundry purposes when touring in the outback. Lay the spare tyre on the ground or on a rock, spread canvas over, press it in and fill the depression with water. Safe, clean and easier to carry than a tub, large bucket or basin, and the wheel is always with you.

❖

Build a small guesthouse down the back paddock or back yard instead of renting a holiday cottage, and give yourself a short holiday at home. It saves a lot of money and there's no need for travelling.

Instead of putting tea in a thermos flask, boil the milk and water together and put this into the flask; then make a very strong cup of tea and put this into a bottle. By putting a little of the strong tea in a cup and adding the hot milk and water mixture, you get a nicer cup of tea on your picnic or outing.

When out camping, put unpeeled bananas into the coals of your fire to taste the pleasure of real, natural food.

❖

A thermos flask carried on a sea voyage is invaluable for holding cold water in the tropics. The cabin steward will fill it daily, if required, and one can always be sure of a cool drink in the cabin.

❖

Make oilcoth or baize slips for your cushions before going on a holiday tour. You will not have to worry about the ground being damp, and a soapy cloth keeps them looking like new.

❖

Keep the moths from your bathers during the winter by placing the perfectly dry costume in a screw-top Mason jar.

If you live in a lonely, isolated place with little opportunity for social evenings, dress up for your radio entertainment at home. A quick warm to cool shower, a liberal shake of your favourite talcum powder, clean undies and a nice frock, and instead of the family drudge, a dainty leisured lady is ready to enjoy the evening's offering of music, comedy or drama. It may startle the family at first, but it acts as an example.

Instead of carrying toilet soap when travelling, pack a tube of shaving cream. No waste, no wet cake of soap and delightfully refreshing to use.

❖

When going away for a holiday, put a little lavender oil on a few saucers and place them in some of the rooms. This will destroy any moths in the house and the usual musty smell or 'shut-up' atmosphere will be absent on your return.

❖

Afternoon tea beneath a large spreading tree is delightful, but it is tiresome when the cloth keeps blowing up. To overcome this, cut four large flowers from gay-coloured cretonne and appliqué to each corner of the picnic cloth, leaving the top of each flower open to form a pocket. Then, when you set the table, drop a lar-gish smooth river stone into each pocket. Pack the stones in the picnic basket so you always have them with you.

❖

Keep your butter cool for a picnic in this way. Soak a brick in cold water, wrap it in a wet cloth and place it in the shade. The evaporation of the water will keep the brick cold, and the butter placed upon it will be kept as cool and firm as though it were on ice.

Just before leaving by train or car for a long journey, wipe your face with a pad of cottonwool moistened with witch hazel to which has been added a few drops of eau de Cologne. Dry with another pad of cottonwool and then use the powder puff. This avoids using hard or lime-rich water so damaging to fine complexions.

❖

Don't put heavy photographs or vases – particularly those full of water – on top of your piano. They not only tend to scratch the surface, but they deaden the tone.

❖

❖

If, while travelling or away from home, you have a squeaky handle or rusty catch on your suitcase, rub a dab of face cream onto the offending item. I oiled the hinges on a cabin door aboard the *Edinburgh Castle* with face cream and enjoyed the journey between England and Africa much better for doing so!

❖

In hot weather, keep a piece of blotting paper cut to the shape of an insole inside each shoe to absorb perspiration of the feet. This saves the stockings from becoming hard and difficult to wash. Renew the paper frequently.

❖

A brick soaked in kerosene and packed in a leakproof container will quickly start the campfire even if the wood is not quite dry.

Avoid a sun-peeled nose at the beach. Cut or tear a piece of paper – newspaper will do – into the outline of a plump fig, fold down the centre lengthwise and tuck the tapered end under the bridge of your specs or sunglasses. This cowl fits snugly and protects the nose at all angles.

❖

Should you have to travel a good deal by train at night, machine-sew a good thick rug at the two selvedge edges and along one end. This 'sleep' bag won't keep falling off in the night; you won't feel the draughts as you can put it right up over your head.

What a Good Idea!

❖

The generation of women that withstood the hard years of World War I and, later, the Depression of the 1930s, had learnt much from their parents and grandparents by way of economy and practicality which would serve them well. In their world, a penny saved was a penny earned, and they recycled and re-used in creative and innovative ways.

It was an era in which the kitchen linoleum was a costly outlay and had to be re-used when no longer suitable for the kitchen, and when hats were so frequently worn that they eventually wore out. Very little was thrown away in any sphere of life: if it could not be mended, it was used for another purpose. These women were not afraid to pick up a hammer, nor to take up the carpet. They could transform gum leaves into Christmas cards, devise amazing pieces of household equipment and even make their own lino! They could (and did) turn their hands to anything, from repairing the wash copper to packing the furniture on moving day, and their ingenuity made the task far easier.

The spirit of 'do it yourself' and of making do with available resources thrived in these times. The hints in this chapter reveal the self-sufficiency and independence of the era and the qualities and strengths of the redoubtable women whose resourcefulness was always directed to improving the quality of life of their families.

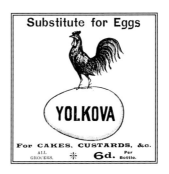

To lengthen blankets that have shrunk in the washing, machine a band of strong material on one end. Tuck this band in at the foot of the bed, leaving the entire blanket length for the top of the bed. This is especially suitable for use on children's beds.

❖

The working life of an old floor-mop can be lengthened if you slip an old knitted beret over it and polish with that. The beret can be easily washed and it imparts a splendid shine to the floor.

❖

USES FOR OLD FELT HATS

Old felt hats are invaluable for making insoles for shoes that have worn thin. These hats can also be cut in strips to make wicks for your hurricane lamps. Soak the strips in oil until needed. Save the brims of brightly coloured velour and felt hats; they are ideal for making into many attractive novelties for fetes.

❖

Use corrugated cardboard on the treads under the stair-carpet when you cannot afford underfelt. Put it on the stairs in three layers. When finally trodden down quite flat it can be easily and cheaply renewed.

Make good long-lasting dishcloths from parcel string that has been knitted loosely on big wooden needles. These can be washed and boiled, look so much better than bits of rags, and are good scourers.

❖

If you take up the old kitchen lino, cut the remaining good parts into a new floor-covering for the outhouse; cover the front of the thunder box also. There is much good wear left in the lino for this purpose.

When shoe polish becomes dry, hold the tin over the steam from a boiling kettle for a few minutes; it will quickly become moist, allowing you to use the very last bit.

❖

When a frying pan develops a small leak, cut off the portion opposite the handle, paint the pan with any paint desired and you have a neat and serviceable 'dust-pan' that will last for years.

❖

Throw your soap suds from wash-day over the lemon, grapefruit or orange tree. This will help to keep the aphids away.

Don't throw away a bucket or dish if it springs a leak. Mend it with a press-stud fastener, one half inside, the other outside, and tap it lightly with a hammer to fasten the press-stud. A teapot can be mended the same way.

❖

If you have an old pair of slippers with goods soles but worn out tops, knit with any old wool a big enough piece to fit over the top. Sew the knitted piece onto the upper of the slipper.

❖

Buy tea-towels by the dozen and all one size. When they begin to wear thin, sew two of them together along all four edges and have another three months wear from them.

❖

Every time you cut bread, place the board on a clean sheet of paper and collect the crumbs. Keep in a jar and use for fish, cutlets and rissoles.

❖

ECONOMICAL HOT WATER

Never grill or make toast on the gas stove without standing a kettle or saucepan of water on the top. Generally, by the time the chops or steak are cooked, the kettle is almost boiling. If hot water is not needed at once, fill two thermos flasks or fill the hot water bottle to have warm water for washing before bed.

Half a teaspoon of glycerine worked into the surface of a rubber-stamp pad will temporarily restore the usefulness of the pad, whatever colour it is. Rub the glycerine in with the back of a knife.

❖

Re-string pearls or valuable beads on a mandolin E-string, which costs only a few pence and will never break or cut.

❖

Keep all your scraps of bread and dry them in the oven when you are baking. Store for crumbing cutlets, brains, fish and so on.

❖

If the hot-water bottle has outlived its usefulness, take out the stopper, fill the bag with kapok or other filling, and replace the stopper with a tight-fitting cork. It makes a handy kneeling pad for floor polishing, or in the garden.

❖

Eggs can be kept fresh for up to five months by gathering them three times a day and immediately giving them a liberal coating of melted beeswax – not hot, just melted – Pack them into small boxes and store in a cool place. You are never short of eggs this way.

❖

To remove face powder from a black coat, mix a teaspoon of ammonia with enough salt to make a soft mixture. Rub the place using a soft cloth.

MR A. HIGGINSON & MISS CARRIE MOORE

When your schoolgirl daughter is in a hurry and there's no time to press the crumpled hair-ribbon, tie it round the kettle of boiling water, or the teapot. The wrinkles will smooth out quickly.

❖

For the bigger figure: put your skirt on a three-inch wide elastic band instead of a petersham band and walk in comfort.

❖

To dry a beret after washing and keep it in shape, slip a teaplate inside the cap and place it in the sun. Press with a slightly damp cloth.

❖

When your white shoes have reached the stage when nothing seems to clean them satisfactorily, wash them with a cloth soaked in equal parts of methylated spirits and ammonia. The result is amazing, and there is no need to use cleaner immediately.

❖

If a cotton sheet is placed between two blankets, it will give more warmth than four blankets, as the cotton retains the warmth.

When packing furniture for removal, protect the legs of chairs and tables by pulling old stockings over them; cover backs of chairs with pillowcases, which can easily be washed when you arrive at your destination.

❖

GUM LEAVES

Some time prior to a party or wedding, select large gum leaves and press until firm but still green. Then, with silver or gold paint, write on each the name of the guest. These are especially appreciated by overseas visitors. Alternatively, trace a large gum leaf on to a piece of window-blind linen and cut out. With a soft brush, give the traced leaves a thin coat of Windsor and Newton's colours, shading from the stem with red-brown to green, and yellow on the tip. Thin the paint with a few drops of eucalyptus oil to give it the true gum leaf smell and a natural gloss. When dry write a motto on each leaf in gold ink. They make good birthday or Christmas cards and book-marks and last for years.

Never throw away sardine-tin 'keys' after use. Unroll the tin, scald the key and keep it. As a bodkin this tool is admirable; sharpened it becomes an awl, and it will lever off patent bottle-stoppers. It has many other uses.

❖

AUNTY KATE'S HOME-MADE LINO

This lino lasted many years and was far better than the 'dirt' floor of Aunty Kate's day. Her lino was envied by many, but copied by few. It took time and great ingenuity to make – all this while rearing a largish family, cooking on a fuel stove, washing in a fuel copper, milking the cows, chopping the wood, making everyone's clothes and driving the horses and buggy to cover the many miles she had to travel to collect some of the provisions she was not able to grow or make herself.

Measure the required length and width of good quality hessian. Glue large sheets of newspaper layer by layer by layer over the hessian, and lastly glue large sheets of strong brown paper over the newspaper. When this is dry and firm, paint it the desired colour with a good 'walk-upon' paint. Then, with an egg cup, and a small tea-cup, make circles on the painted surface and paint these circles in various colours to suit yourself.

❖

A mousetrap makes a good paperclip for travellers, truck drivers or others who have to carry and refer to papers while driving. Detach the bait plate and setting wire, and attach the trap to the dashboard of the truck, or fix it to a convenient place on the car. Paint it a bright colour if desired.

❖

When cleaning pictures and putting them back into their frames, bind the picture to the glass with passepartout binding, then fix to the frame. No dust or dirt can get in to spoil the photograph or etching.

A short 'reading aloud' by the fireside on a winter's evening by members of an adolescent family helps the break up the 'lone hunter out for amusement' attitude that is intruding on family life. Choose short magazine articles of general interest.

❖

A large bead, such as is used on milk-jug covers, makes an ideal shoe-button in an emergency.

A VERY HANDY MEASURE

A kerosene tin holds 4 gallons of liquid; 18 pounds of pollard; 12 pounds of bran; 30 pounds of whole wheat; 28 pounds of whole maize, and 25 pounds of cracked maize. If you are selling your produce, even to buyers passing through, these measures are easy and convenient.

Pictures will always hang straight if a strip of sandpaper, about half an inch wide, is glued near the lower edge of the frame at the back. This grips the wall and keeps the frame in position.

❖

Have your worn-out lawn-mower converted into a trolley similar to those used on railway stations for baggage. On washday, place your clothes basket and pegs on it and simply wheel it to the line.

❖

A folding camp stool is a great convenience in a small guest room. It is a comfortable height for unpacking a suitcase and when not needed can be folded and put in a wardrobe.

❖

Before putting your work basket away, thread three needles, one with white, one with black, the third with darning wool. This is quick and handy for mother if she needs to sew a button on or mend a rent in a hurry.

If you need only a little lemon juice, pierce a hole in the lemon with a steel knitting needle and squeeze. The hole will close up and the lemon remain fresh.

❖

Old lace curtains, beyond mending and washed free of starch, make the finest window cleaners. They never leave any lint on glass and give an excellent polish.

❖

When a small leak starts in a copper, a hammer blow will often effect a lasting repair. Lay solid iron against the spot and hammer it as if riveting. The hole will close up and stay put.

❖

If calfskin or kid gloves get wet, rub a tiny drop of castor oil well in while they are still on your hands. This prevents them from drying hard and stiff.

❖

When wearing a 'best dress' and the dishes have to be washed after a meal, protect long sleeves by pulling over them old long stockings with the feet cut off.

❖

When washing and rinsing coloured materials, add a teaspoon of Epsom salts to the water; it will prevent the most delicate fabrics from fading or running.